TIME AND
INFORMATION
MANAGEMENT
THAT REALLY WORKS!

Other books in this series include:

Office Design That Really Works!
Computer Office Setup That Really Works!
Business Communication That Really Works!

Managing Editor: Howard A. Cohl
Project Management: Mari Florence, Lynette Padwa
Composition and Layout: Wendy Loreen
Production Editor: Nancy McKinley

Printed in Mexico

Cover Photograph: Comstock, Inc.
Illustration and Photo Credits: Page 118

Library of Congress Cataloging-in-Publication Data
        Allen, Kathleen R., Ph.D.
        Time and Information Management That Really Works!.
           128 p. 28 cm.

        ISBN 1-886111-22-7
        1. Business.   2. Reference–Business.
94-73450 CIP   1995

1 2 3 4 5 6 7 8 9 10-XX-98 97 96 95

TIME AND INFORMATION MANAGEMENT
THAT REALLY WORKS!

ORGANIZATION FOR THE '90s

KATHLEEN R. ALLEN, Ph.D.
Series Editor: Peter H. Engel

Recommended by
Office DEPOT®

Contents

Contents

Introduction

Welcome to the *Small Business Solutions Series.* This series was designed with one person in mind—you, the small-business owner.

In creating these books, we had three goals. First, we wanted to answer your questions about starting and running a small business. Second, we wanted to provide you with information. Finally, we wanted to help guide your thinking by providing you with sound alternative solutions to many of the problems you are likely to face.

These books deliver the goods by answering the many day-to-day questions that arise in getting a new or existing business up and running smoothly. Lively and colorful, these user-friendly guides are practical, concise and packed with the information you need.

You—and *only* you—know what's best for your business. The *Small Business Solutions Series* offers you a handy reference that allows you to make quick, educated decisions about the countless operating details you must deal with in order to be free to move onto the *real* challenges of growing a business.

I'd like to thank all of the people responsible for this series, particularly my co-authors Kathleen R. Allen and Bonnie Lund.

Good luck in your business!

Peter H. Engel
Series Editor and President, Affinity Publishing, Inc.

Organize and Conquer

Ah, the office of the nineties—that streamlined, paperless office where all facts are on file, formatted, and just a fingertip away. The trendwatchers told us it would be like this. They preached the marvels of computerization and forecast the day when metal file cabinets would find permanent homes at the bottom of the sea as habitats for the fish.

So what went wrong? Why do most people tear around like Dagwood Bumstead, forever losing files, misfiling files, or creating piles instead of files? Why does organizing the office continue to confound us, even though we have all the tools we need to wrestle the beast to the ground?

It's the human factor, of course. Whatever ultrasophisticated tools one may possess, organization is ultimately up to the person using them. That's where this book comes in: to show you the basic principles, strategies, and shortcuts that will demystify business organization and perhaps even make it fun for you. One thing is certain—this book will empower you and save you money. For without a doubt, an organized office is the foundation of a smoothly running, efficient, and effective enterprise.

Why Organize?

The most important commodities in your office that should be well organized are time and information. The better organized your time is, the more you can accomplish, and the more leisure time you'll have to live your life outside of work. As for information, no matter what your business is, information is the fuel that keeps it running—financial data, product tracking, personnel files, project material—the thousands of facts and figures that keep you competitive, solvent, and (if all goes well) profitable.

Information organization is a revealing mirror of your business: it's either under control or it's not. When it's not, panic, wasted time, and lost clients aren't far behind. Perhaps most important, an out-of-control information system sabotages productivity and makes employees feel resentful and angry. Maybe they interpret those missing files as an effort to keep them out of the loop. Or maybe they just see it as evidence of a manager who's not up to the job. Even if your office only has one employee—you—its information system is vital to productivity and professionalism.

But you know all that, at least instinctively. It's the reason you picked up this book. The good news is that the same principles of organization that work for paper-filing systems work for computer-filing systems, for databases, and for virtually all types of information systems. This book will introduce you to those principles, guiding you through the steps you'll need to transform your business from paper salad to a data buffet that serves up exactly what you want, when you want it. And it won't hurt a bit.

Are you lost on the information superhighway?

What do business people have to deal with in this computerized age? Nothing less than an information superhighway, and it's speeding up, not slowing down. The highway is paved not only with bytes but also with good old paper. With the ease and speed of printers, photocopiers, and fax machines, we now produce more paper than ever before—570 billion documents, according to the Association of Records Management. Every year, Americans produce an additional 30 billion, make 350 billion photocopies of the originals, and throw away another 130 billion copies.

It's more difficult to tame an office today than it was ten years ago because we have twice as many documents to organize: the computer version and the hard copy paper version. Why is paper still so important? It has a permanency computer files lack. Paper is still the primary means of communicating complex ideas, legal contracts, manuscripts, memos— nearly everything. People can mark up a paper document, sign it, edit it, and so forth. For this reason, the paperless office remains an unrealized dream.

Can mismanaged information harm your business?

Whether you're drowning in paper or hopelessly tangled in computer files, you're probably aware that mismanaged information makes for frustration and wasted energy. But sloppy information systems are even more insidious than you may realize. They can

☐ lose you business, because you can't meet deadlines, keep appointments straight, or even return phone calls promptly

☐ choke cash flow, because you lack an effective system of keeping track of your money

☐ damage your credit, because you have no plan for paying bills on time

☐ cripple productivity, because you aren't able to store and retrieve information quickly and effectively

☐ stifle creativity, because you can't concentrate on your vision when you're mired in paperwork

What This Book Will Teach You

You must find a way to organize your mountain of information. When you do, you'll save time, money, and effort. You'll even save trees, because once you know how to organize, you'll reduce the amount of paper documents you create. Your mission, then, is to transform your office. This book will teach you how to

- ❏ become more organized
- ❏ think ahead and plan instead of react
- ❏ set business goals and establish routines to achieve them
- ❏ organize your time and use it more productively
- ❏ stop duplicating your efforts so frequently
- ❏ manage the financial end of your business

- ❏ set up your business so that everything it needs to operate efficiently is instantly available
- ❏ develop foolproof filing systems designed especially for your business
- ❏ choose the computer technology most suited to enhance the organization of your particular business

That last item—computer technology—can be a wonderful ally in conquering your information woes. You will learn all about the best tools for your business, from local-area networks to lightweight laptop models. When they're understood and wisely used, these computers can free you and your staff for more productive (and enjoyable) pursuits than chasing data and miring yourself down in an information wasteland.

 No Just as important as learning what technology to buy is learning when to say no. This book provides guidelines for choosing both technological and nontechnological aids—tried and true items such as in-boxes. The aim is to buy those tools that will work for your office, not to purchase the biggest, shiniest equipment. It's only worth the money if it makes your business better.

 Every procedure, strategy, and piece of equipment recommended here will have trade-offs in speed, security, cost, and flexibility. In deciding which tools and systems are right for you, remember that efficiency and effectiveness are at the heart of most successful business efforts. *Efficiency* refers to completing a task with the least possible amount of wasted labor, cash, or time; *effectiveness* refers to the quality of the work. Balancing the two is an art worth learning.

Efficiency versus Effectiveness
A woman who ran a referral service for tutors was intent on keeping all her sources confidential. She didn't want the tutors running out and starting their own small referral businesses. All the source information, therefore, was accessible to her alone; not even her secretary could open those files. This system was very effective in maintaining control over the information, but it required her to be in the office to personally handle clients' requests. Every time she was out of the office, the business was put on hold. Obviously, this was not a very efficient way of maintaining control—it cost her too many clients. Ultimately she devised a better system: a portable phone, laptop computer, and modem allowed her to access information and return client calls from outside the office.

The Price of Information

Information is a resource that has a cost associated with it. Once you understand this, you'll be able to appreciate how the way you manage information can either boost your profits or reduce them.

The cost of information is determined by four factors:

- ❑ degree of accuracy
- ❑ speed of access
- ❑ frequency of update
- ❑ opportunity cost

If you need information that is more accurate, easier to get at, and is used more frequently, you'll pay more for it. But that additional cost must be weighed against the cost to your business of not having what you need.

 Degree of accuracy. The more accurate your information, the more it costs. Suppose your bookkeeper is reconciling the books for the month and discovers a two-dollar discrepancy. Do you tell her to spend another several hours looking for the error or instruct her simply to adjust the imbalance? The wise business person—indeed, the one who will stay in business—quickly recognizes that it makes more sense to adjust the imbalance. It's an example of trading total accuracy for better use of your employee's time, which in this case is far more effective and efficient.

 Speed of access. The faster you need information, the more it's likely to cost you. By the same token, the more quickly you can access information, the more quickly you can achieve your goal—and the more competitive you become. Computer technology is the most cost-effective way to give you speedy access to information and the ability to quickly respond to clients' requests. Computers also enable you to store huge volumes of data and to project various models and scenarios so you may spot potential problems and opportunities in advance. That often translates directly to dollars.

Computer technology puts information at your fingertips.

The Price of Information

Penny-wise and Pound-foolish

One printer resisted computerizing his estimating procedure. It took him 24 hours to bid a job his competitors could bid in two hours. True, the computer and data entry required to set up his estimating system would have been much costlier than the calculator and paper forms he was used to. But he lost many clients by not being able to access information as quickly as his competition.

 Frequency of update. The more frequently you need to update your information, the more it will cost. You may be surprised to learn, for example, how much time the successful manager of a beachfront hotel must spend updating reservations and room availability. Not only does she need instant access to all the information for as much as a year in advance, but she must also be able to network with other hotels in the nearby area. The effectiveness of her operation is made possible by a costly and sophisticated computer system. The trade-offs of expense and time commitment in this case are more than offset by the benefits of increased competiveness, efficiency, and volume of business.

 Opportunity cost. This fourth factor is really a gauge of how important the other three are to you. The cost of information accuracy, speed of access, and frequency of update must always be weighed against the cost of *not* having these commodities. How competitive will you be without them? How much will *not* receiving accurate information quickly cost you in terms of opportunities you will miss and business you will never see?

The Price of Information

Take financial data, for instance. Any business—from neighborhood pizza parlor to petroleum conglomerate—must be acutely aware of its cash status. Its financial-information system must provide the current cash status of the business—usually a cash-flow statement or bank reconciliation statement. This cash status must be available instantly, whether it be through computer files or ledger books. Finally, the financial data must be current and updated on a regular basis every day, week, or month.

The opportunity cost of not having such a system in place would be severe, if not devastating. The company would not be able to make purchasing decisions, payroll decisions, or any other decisions, because it wouldn't know how much money it had. A company that neglects this financial-information system is playing Russian roulette with its future. Analysis of opportunity cost is also vital to a well-run department. A manager will lose business and incur unnecessary costs if he or she does not have quick access to accurate information.

The Price of Information

? What is the bottom line?

In some cases, not getting fast, accurate, and frequent information may cost you your business itself. That's why, although some tools (such as computers and software) may be expensive, the right technology combined with carefully thought-out organizational strategies is priceless.

Consider speaking with colleagues and competitors to see what types of systems meet their needs and are best suited to their line of work. Systems consultants can help you get started and provide you with a setup tailored to your business parameters.

With all the technology currently available, you may find yourself with more recommendations than you can shuffle through. Sit down and prioritize your needs and then build a system from the bottom up.

No information system is entirely foolproof, but by understanding exactly what your needs are and how your system works, you can stay well ahead of the game and navigate most of the rough waters that come with running a business.

? Is there such a thing as too much information?

For decades, business pundits and the media predicted that the more information people would have access to, the better off they'd be. But while information gives people much more power to move effectively in the business world, dealing with mountains of data can be an enormous burden. Fearing that they may be unequipped to make wise business decisions, many people compulsively collect articles, magazines, books, disks, and tapes. While some are truly information junkies who enjoy having lots of facts on hand, most people hoard information because they don't know how to process it or to determine what's important and what's not. At some point, they stop trying to process it altogether, feeling entirely overwhelmed by the task. That condition is commonly called information overload, and it may work against your commitment to organize your business. The following pointers will help you deal with the problem of too much data.

Conquering Information Overload

 Better decisions do not result from more information. While you do need a certain amount of information to make informed decisions, most people are bombarded with much more than they can handle. The result: They make decisions on a fraction of the information that is available to them. Does it matter? In some cases it does, but research does *not* support the theory that more information is better. The amount of information you need should be gauged by the type of decision you're making. Routine decisions require little information; complex decisions require more. The key is in knowing what information is needed and how to get it quickly—and that's where organizational systems come in.

 Don't be intimidated by the amount of information available on computers. As a business owner or manager you probably spend more of your time talking to people than to computers. You communicate orally over the phone, in meetings, in the hall, over coffee.

And until that day when you can carry on an intelligent conversation with your computer, you will continue to gather most of the information you use from other human beings. In general, computers provide data—data that need to be analyzed by people. Just as you pick and choose books to read in the library, you should pick and choose from computers only the information you really need.

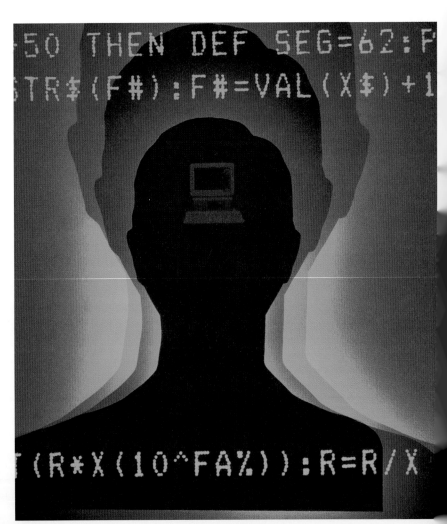

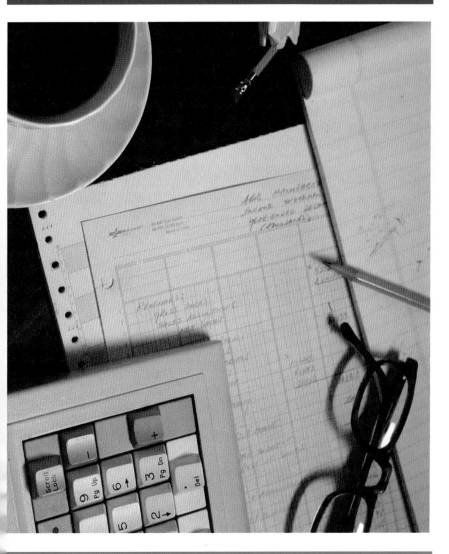

Get to know your management-information system. Any time you don't understand a major aspect of your business and must rely on the intelligence and integrity of someone else, you make yourself extremely vulnerable. Embezzlement, piracy, and plain old incompetence could quite easily destroy all your hard work, and it wouldn't take long to happen. For that reason, you should either create your business's management-information system yourself or actively monitor the person doing so (inputting the program, setting up the systems, and so forth). *Do not let someone else create and control your management-information system.* No one knows or cares about your business or department the way you do. You must be completely comfortable with the information sources that keep the wheels turning, and the money flowing, in your enterprise.

Information is the lifeblood of your business—you must make yourself intimately familiar with it. You can't let mere data confound or intimidate you. But no matter how overwhelmed you may have felt in the past, in these pages you'll learn how to cull the information you need from all the sources available to you and how to channel it exactly the way you want.

Dynamics of Office Organization

There are those people who love to organize and who seem to have a natural talent for it, and then there is everyone else, whose organizational abilities fall somewhere between passable and disastrous. You probably already have a sense of how organized you are—no doubt someone at some point has commented on your extraordinary organizational skills or lack of them. Of course, *organized* is a subjective term. What is organization to one person is chaos to another, and that dynamic is at the heart of many mismanaged offices.

It's up to you, as the owner or manager, to set the organizational stage for your employees and co-workers and to make certain that all the players are reading from the same script. Otherwise, each empoyee will organize in his or her individual style. In some respects this is understandable, since each employee handles different aspects of the business—payroll, fulfillment, research and development—and each requires access to different types of information.

But the combination of individual organizational styles and individual functions can be like a time bomb. From the outside the business looks fine, but in reality it is operating like a group of independent mini-businesses at cross purposes instead of one integrated business with a unified goal. As long as members of the business team remain constant in their roles, no one realizes that a system problem exists. Then one day the accounts payable clerk leaves to take a better job. Naturally, with her goes the key to deciphering the filing system and finding out what bills need to be paid. Chaos ensues as everyone scrambles to crack the code. The business has now lost valuable time and money. Clearly, a system that can be understood and used by everybody will make your business or office more efficient—and ultimately bring you more success.

Dynamics of Office Organization

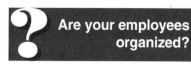

Are your employees organized?

Take advantage of those staffers who have an innate sense of organization as these people can be key individuals on your information management team. If you are starting from scratch, meet with your employees and ask for organizational suggestions. If their ideas fit with your way of doing business, try to implement their suggestions into your overall operations. This way, your employees feel that they have a vested interest in the company.

Most people could probably stand to improve the efficiency and effectiveness of their business. However, in the day-to-day running of the business, it's often difficult to find time to evaluate organizational systems that are already established. It's easy to assume the business is running the best that it can—until something goes wrong and you have to react to a crisis. A far better plan is to take a good long look right now at how your office or business is run and decide whether your information systems are shipshape or leaky.

The following quiz will give you a snapshot of the current status of your system. You might want to make copies of the quiz and ask your employees or co-workers to take it as well. Their input will offer you a different perspective and ensure that the system you develop has a good chance of succeeding.

How Organized Are You?

1.	You don't return phone calls in a timely fashion.	True	False
2.	You can't find what you need when you need it.	True	False
3.	You feel that you are losing control of your work.	True	False
4.	You have stacks of paper everywhere.	True	False
5.	You don't have a life outside of work.	True	False
6.	You don't know how to say no.	True	False
7.	You don't know how much money you have.	True	False
8.	Your work is constantly interrupted.	True	False
9.	You are often late to meetings and appointments.	True	False
10.	You have overdue bills stacking up because you haven't had the time to get to them.	True	False

Answering *true* to any of these statements may indicate you have a weakness that could adversely affect your productivity. But don't despair; you're not alone. According to statistics developed by the Wilson Learning Institute of Minnesota, about half the people in the United States are what could be charitably characterized as less than organized.

Improving Your Natural Skills

? What's your organizational personality?

It seems each of us, for reasons no one truly understands, makes a choice at an early age to solve our problems and cope with our lives in one of two ways: by collecting, organizing, and analyzing data, or by discussing the situation with other people. Neither one is right or wrong; there are strengths and weaknesses inherent in each choice.

When starting a new project or tackling a problem, what is your first inclination? Do you dig into the data, or do you get up and go talk it over with a friend? Do you rely on logic or gut feelings? Do you believe the facts will lead you to the proper course of action, or do you distrust data, suspecting that those wicked little numbers can be twisted to prove anything at all?

Use What You Have
Don't be hard on yourself if organization isn't your strong suit. An easy way to improve is to keep a lined pad of paper on your desk and jot down ideas. Seeing these words will improve their order in your head.

? How can a people-oriented person improve efficiency?

If you are the intuitive, shoot-from-the-hip type, you probably did not do very well on our quiz, and you probably could use some help getting organized. There's nothing wrong with you. Your skill with people has seen you through difficult times and is a big reason you've gotten as far as you have. But time management is most likely not one of your strengths.

Ask for advice from colleagues whose organizational skills you admire.

Why do people-oriented individuals have a hard time with efficiency? One theory holds that it's because they are usually big talkers. Unfortunately, verbal communication is the least reliable way of transmitting information. To prove this, give someone a series of instructions, or tell him or her a story or joke, then have that individual tell someone else what you said. Have the second person tell a third, and have the third tell a fourth. Now, ask the final person in the chain to tell you what you said. You'll be amazed at how distorted your original words have become.

Improving Your Natural Skills

When this game of "telephone" is unintentionally played out on a daily basis, it's a tremendous time drain. Force yourself to write memos instead—and make those memos as clear and to the point as possible. To keep the telephone game under control, copy everyone who's likely to be affected by the memo's information.

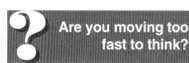

Are you moving too fast to think?

An English businessman was heard to say, "The reason Americans do more than the Brits is because in America actions are unimpeded by thought." Is that you? Do you dash full speed ahead even if you don't know where you're going? Would you rather *do* than think?

To find out, try this simple test: Select a problem that has bothered you for a long while. Sit down, get comfortable, and clear your mind of everything else. When you're ready, note the exact time, and now—think. Don't talk to anyone. Don't look up anything in your files. Don't make notes. Just sit and think. If you get restless by the five-minute mark and are climbing the walls before ten minutes have elapsed, your natural impulse to go, go, go may be robbing you of your greatest asset—the richness of your own mind.

Discipline yourself to slow down and *really* think. It won't be easy for you. If an idea doesn't come to you immediately, you'll feel like you're wasting time and feel compelled to do something, anything. But remember this: The biggest waste of time is redoing a task that wasn't thoroughly thought out and done well the first time. By keeping this in mind, you'll be more inclined to think your idea through before jumping in unprepared.

Environmental Load and Overload

Learn to Respect the Details

If you take to details like a duck takes to the desert, you must force yourself to dig into the data. Taking action without the facts is nothing more than a guessing game, and, in the end, it's a game you can't win.

? How can the highly organized person improve?

Believe it or not, the Englishman quoted above actually meant his remark as a compliment. He went on to explain that, in his opinion, many of his countrymen suffer from analysis-paralysis, which leads to endless discussion but very little action.

Highly organized people can fall into this trap. They can spend far too much time organizing and analyzing, and not nearly enough time doing. To such individuals the advice is: Stop thinking about doing it, and just do it!

As you consider which course of action will best combat your own time-management problems, remember that your behavior is only one factor contributing to the overall efficiency of your business. Another factor is environmental overload.

? What is environmental load and overload?

The quantity of information a business processes and the degree of variety in the type of information is called **environmental load.** The more uncertainty, complexity, and deadlines a business faces in processing information and conducting its business, the higher its environmental load.

Start-up and rapidly growing businesses usually face more pressure than mature businesses. As environmental load increases to the point that it exceeds the business's ability to deal with it, a breakdown in the operations of the business occurs—**environmental overload.** This explains why too rapid growth spells death for so many businesses. The information systems that were developed to meet the needs of a small young business may not be able to handle the increasing environmental load brought on by rapid growth. Research indicates that there is a strong relationship between a business owner's ability to build and manage information systems and the business' ability to grow and reach its goals.

Businesses generally respond to environmental overload in one of two ways: They give up and do not respond to the situation at all—"I can't meet the deadline; we'll just have to lose the sale." Or, in frustration and panic, they act on whatever information they *do* have on hand, even if it's insufficient.

Environmental Load and Overload

Too Little Information, Too Late

A young entrepreneur created an educational product designed to help kids learn U.S. geography. Sales were slow at first as he searched for the best vehicle to get his product to the target market—the public schools. His organizational system was simple and met the needs of his start-up venture, and he had the luxury of time to develop procedures as he went along. Eventually he managed to get an agreement with a major publisher of maps and atlases to market and distribute his product. He was on his way!

Then one Friday he received an order for 1,000 maps that had to be delivered on Monday, in time for a statewide book fair. He realized to his dismay that his business's information system was ill-equipped to handle the pressure of this sudden increase in demand. He needed temporary employees to work through the weekend, but because he hadn't developed a listing of freelance workers, he had to call a high-priced agency to supply the manpower. The biggest crisis involved shipping. The maps had to be rush-shipped Sunday night, and the entrepreneur had no idea which delivery service offered the best rates on large bulk shipments. His assistant had researched the subject months ago, but his notes were nowhere to be found, and he had never created a computer file or report of his findings. The assistant himself was away for the weekend. Overwhelmed, the entrepreneur called his regular shipping company, shut his eyes, and signed the bill.

Features of Business Owners

What if you own a business?

Before delving into organizational strategies, consider one last essential reason for creating a first-rate management-information system: the nature of being a business owner. Business owners tend to display four general characteristics.

Business owners work long hours at a variety of tasks.
Research has found that the number of hours you work increases in direct proportion to your level of responsibility within the business. As the owner of the business, you carry the most responsibility for its success and tend to spend more hours in business-related activities. The better your office is organized, the more effectively you'll be able to carry out your myriad duties and the more leisure time you may create for yourself.

A business owner's work is varied and fragmented. You are generally involved in a variety of different activities throughout the day and therefore spend relatively little time on any one thing. So you must be able to process—and access—a great amount of information that is inherently diverse in nature.

The work of the business owner tends to be primarily verbal.
The higher up in the business hierarchy you are, the more time you spend in meetings and on the telephone. Likewise, as your business grows and you take on more employees to do the routine work, you are able to spend more time planning, investigating, coordinating, evaluating, negotiating, and so on. In all these activities it is vital to have business information instantly at hand.

Features of Business Owners

The business owner tends to spend as much or more time outside the organization as inside. As you acquire more staff to take care of the day-to-day operations of the business, you are freer to conduct the networking activities that will help your business grow: new sales contacts, new financing sources, new opportunities. Exchanging information with people at all levels is one of the key characteristics of business owners.

Whether or not you own your business, the way you organize its flow of information and the way you manage the time you spend at work is crucial to your success. It all begins with an obvious but often neglected task: setting goals.

The old warning, "If you don't know where you're going, any road will get you there," has special meaning for business people. Your business is not the place to lay back and see where the river takes you. Most likely it will take you over a cliff unless you're fully in charge of the canoe, have a specific destination, and anticipate the water hazards and good fishing spots along the way.

"But of course I have a goal," you may object. "I own Tweedledee Egg Farm. My goal is to sell eggs." That isn't really a goal, it's a *raison d'etre*—reason for existing. Goals are long-term objectives that guide your daily decision making. They are the accomplishments by which you judge whether you have achieved success, both in your business and on a personal level. Goals are necessary to effectively focus your time and energy on the task at hand.

The pointers on the next pages will help you set basic goals for your business.

Goal-Setting Basics

Are your goals measurable?

If you don't set measurable goals, you'll have a hard time figuring out how to achieve them. For instance, suppose you set a goal to "make more money." How do you begin to implement it? By setting another goal to work harder? That goal is just as vague as the first one. But if you set a goal to increase sales by $10,000 in the coming year, you give yourself parameters within which you can make some decisions as to how to proceed.

This step also will enable you to know *when* you have achieved what you set out to do and will make it harder for you to rationalize a failure into a success. Achieving your goals will be more meaningful, therefore, encouraging you to take on more challenges and set further goals for your business.

It's extremely important to be able to congratulate yourself when you've achieved your goal. If you can't tell when you've reached a goal, you never get a sense of accomplishment. Instead, an endless road of work stretches out before you, with very little psychological reward. For business owners this is especially treacherous. You can end up feeling discouraged when in reality you're accomplishing a lot—you just have no way of measuring your efforts.

How will your goals affect your personal life?

Suppose your business goal is to build your market share on a national level. This ambitious goal will require a significant amount of time and effort on your part. Now suppose that one of your personal goals is to spend more time with your family. The conflict here is obvious. You'll need to set some priorities and re-examine one or both of your goals. This isn't to say that you can't have both, but there's likely to be a trade-off somewhere—there are only so many hours in the day.

Try to be as realistic as possible about this issue of family versus work. Look back and honestly assess how much time your work goals have consumed in past years. Naturally, you'll need to talk over your goals with your family. While they may not be able to offer insight on how long it takes you to achieve business goals, they can tell you what their schedules will be like in the upcoming months. If your kids' school and your spouse's job will keep them extra busy, your efforts to spend more time with the family may be futile anyway. Or you may discover that your child has been counting on your help with an especially tough math class this semester. This decision is one you can't make alone.

23

Goal-Setting Basics

 Have you prioritized your goals?

No doubt you'll have more than one goal for your business (and your personal life as well). It helps to rank your goals in order of importance so that you don't scatter your efforts and resources in too many directions. You may be able to work on more than one goal at a time, but if you have determined which goal is most important, you can focus the majority of your time on that one—and increase your chances of reaching it.

Two Goal-Keeping Tips

Set deadlines for your goals. A deadline helps keep you moving forward and makes it less likely that you'll abandon the goal or procrastinate too long.

Put your goals in writing. Visually reviewing your goals somehow makes them more real. Be sure to look at your written goals every day to reinforce your commitment to the project and your business.

Once you know where you want to go, you must figure out how to get there. Achieving a goal may entail not only *doing things* but also *not doing some things.* Pencil and paper in hand, you should

❐ make a list of all the tasks that need to be accomplished for you to reach your goal by the deadline you have set.

❐ make another list of all the activities you can either discard or give to someone else to do. For example, you may decide to say no to some social events and hire a personal assistant to take care of your routine administrative work.

After you've broken down your goal into tasks, you need to do an in-depth reality check to determine if you can really meet the deadlines you've set. This reality check is called a **task analysis.** In addition to clarifying how long each task will take, it will help you prioritize the tasks.

What is task analysis?

Let's take a simple example first. Suppose that one afternoon you need to see a couple of clients, stop at the bank, and visit the office-supply warehouse to pick up some computer supplies. You probably won't be able to complete all of these tasks, so you must prioritize. If you have appointments with the clients, those obviously go at the top of the priority list and will also define where you will be at specific times. You must decide which of the other two tasks gets done first based on whether or not the bank closes early and if either of these stops is close to one of your client appointments.

For more complex and important goals, the steps below will help you analyze the tasks involved.

Analyzing Complex Goals

1. Determine how long it will take to accomplish each task. Measure the time in hours, days, or weeks, depending on the size and complexity of the goal.

2. Designate the start and completion dates for each task.

3. Decide which tasks are critical and must be completed precisely as scheduled to meet the target deadline.

4. Decide how long the noncritical tasks can be delayed before they affect your ability to meet the deadline.

5. Set up a task analysis chart to make sure you can still meet the deadline you've set for yourself. The chart on the next page displays a simple example of the activities leading to the goal of obtaining a loan to buy a small business.

Task Analysis Chart

Activity	Description	Immediately Preceding Task
A	Make a list of financing sources.	
B	Analyze the financial records of the business you wish to buy.	
C	Examine the operations of the business.	
D	Create a business plan for the new business.	B, C
E	Submit the business plan and a proposal for a loan to purchase the new business.	A, D

From this chart you can see that:

❏ Task A (locating financing sources) is an activity that can go on simultaneously with the other tasks that must be accomplished before submitting the proposal to the lender.

❏ Task B (analyzing financial records) and Task C (examining the operations) can go on simultaneously but must be completed before Task E (writing the business plan).

❏ The critical tasks are Tasks B and C. If they are not completed on time, movement toward the goal is delayed. Knowing this, you may want to assign enough people to these tasks to ensure that they are completed in the time allotted. (This may be one of those trade-offs between efficiency and effectiveness, because you'll probably pay more to have the tasks completed quickly.)

Hot Tip

Ken Blanchard, author of the very successful book, The One-Minute Manager, *suggests that you do at least one task every day that will take you closer to your goal. That way you'll avoid the natural tendency to put off tasks until the last possible moment.*

Analyzing and prioritizing the tasks at hand enables your business to run more efficiently.

? How does task analysis help you?

Doing this task analysis gives you the information you need to move ahead. In the case above, for instance, you might decide to push your deadline back so that you have a better chance of successfully meeting it. Why not just delay the deadline later, if it looks like you won't make it? Because the best course of action is to plan realistically *now.* That way the rest of your business won't get neglected as you race to try to meet an unmeetable date. And there's another, more subtle reason: unrealistic deadlines set you up for failure, which can sabotage your enthusiasm and confidence.

? How do you put a price to the tasks?

Again, honesty is invaluable here. Don't underestimate how much of your time a task will take, and remember that your time is money. Does it make more sense to hire someone else to research financing sources? Are you willing to pay a premium in order to have the task completed quickly? Some tasks are more costly than others because they are complex and by their very nature take more time to complete, such as the due diligence on the operations of the new business. For every task, write down a cost estimate, and keep that estimate in mind as you proceed toward your goal.

4 Organizing Time

You've set your goals, and you've analyzed how long each will take, right down to charting out the critical-task paths of the more complex projects. You're glad you did it, but you may be thinking, "It sure took a lot of time." Your time is precious without a doubt. That's why it is imperative to organize it now. This planning time will be paid back to you in large dividends of time saved, money saved, and hassles avoided.

Remarkably, some people don't make a conscious connection between organizing time and organizing information systems, yet the two are closely linked. In this chapter you'll learn to streamline your daily routine and organize your time. Then, when you get into filing systems, computer technology, and all the other data that need managing, you'll have a workable schedule in place and will be able to put your new organizational skills to use immediately.

Time management begins with understanding how time works in your life. First, look at your daily habits and routines.

? **How do routines affect your work?**

If you closely examine a typical day in your life, you'll notice it is full of habits and routines, most of which you've established unconsciously. Some of these are enjoyable and productive, like reading a book for twenty minutes before you fall asleep. Others you'd probably like to get rid of if you could. One thing is nearly always true: it is easier to acquire habits than it is to give them up.

What is the difference between a habit and a routine? A *habit* is a behavior you conduct regularly and without thought, such as putting on the left sock before you put on the right. A *routine* is a customary procedure for doing something, such as a series of calls you might make before determining if a customer is a good credit risk. The two terms are very similar, but the word routine implies some forethought, whereas people usually develop habits unconsciously. Both habits and routines can be changed (and improved).

Creating a Routine

At work, routines ensure that certain tasks get accomplished. Once you've established a routine, it becomes second nature. In that way, routines enable you to get your job done without consciously considering every step.

Are your routines efficient?

Take a few moments to identify the routines you have established in your life, particularly those that affect your work. Examine your workday hour by hour and write down a general outline of it. You may find that a routine you have established is inefficient or incompatible with your work style (for instance, breaking for lunch at 12:00 because everyone else does, even though you get your best work done in the morning and aren't hungry until 1:30).

Or, if you work at home and are a night owl, set up hours during the day that you are available to meet with clients, take phone calls, and interact with the nine-to-five world. Then plan to do your quiet work at night when your natural clock is at high noon.

It's fairly simple to change a routine or establish a new one; what it takes is persistence. The following six-step plan will show you how to do it—but you've got to follow it faithfully.

Create a routine that works best for you.

Creating a Routine

1. **Decide how you want your day to go so that it matches your work and lifestyle.** Picture the perfect day. How would it begin? What would you do? What would you have others do or not do? Although you can't control other people, you can control their impact on you. Once again, consider every hour. Visualize the way your perfect day would unfold. It's important to visualize it, because through doing so you may clarify for yourself what your ideal day should be like.

2. **Write down the pattern you are trying to achieve in the form of an ordered checklist of tasks.** Do you begin your day with a cup of coffee and the newspaper? Add this to your checklist. When do you return phone calls? Review work from the previous day? Make sure the checklist is realistic and applicable to *you*.

3. **Keep that checklist handy; post it where you can easily see it.** The old phrase "out of sight, out of mind" really is true. And when you're trying to establish a new routine, you need to think about it consciously if you're going to make it stick.

4. **Make a concerted effort to follow the new pattern every day.** At the end of the first week, ask yourself if the new routine is working. Are you having an easier time getting started on the first task of the day? Is the routine getting easier to follow?

5. **If you're not satisfied with the new routine, revise it.** Try the revised routine for at least one week.

6. **When you feel comfortable with a pattern, stick to it tenaciously for at least one month.** After a month you should begin to feel comfortable with the new pattern, and can safely vary it now and then. Don't stray too often, however. The more you repeat the pattern, the more habitual (and unconscious) it will become—and thus, the more effective.

Getting Your Routines on Track

How can you change your staff's routines?

It's one thing to train yourself to a new routine; it's quite another to get other people with different work styles to accept your routine or to change their own. But unless you work alone, it's almost inevitable that the changes you make will affect your employees or co-workers.

Even a simple change such as altering the way incoming calls are handled needs to be treated thoughtfully. Should you handle the calls yourself? What are the criteria for your being interrupted to take calls? Should your secretary screen all incoming calls—and how will that affect your relationship with your clients? What about special services offered by the phone company? Could any of them solve the screening problem? Any decision you are considering should be discussed with those whom it will affect. Your staff may be able to offer solutions or point out problems you hadn't considered.

Even if you ask employees for their input, it's not unusual to find resistance to new routines because they generally have become comfortable with the routines already established. The best way to get people to accept a change in routine is to show them how it will benefit *them* as well as you and the business.

What benefits will others reap from efficient routines?

On page 32 you'll find some tips that will help you formulate a few arguments for the changes you want to implement.

Getting Your Routines on Track

 Establishing routines will reduce wasted time. Smart routines streamline an operation so that it takes less time. Once daily tasks are prioritized, they can be accomplished and the next task can be addressed. These routines simplify work for both you and your employees because they structure the workday and eliminate the guesswork for employees.

 Establishing routines will cut down on errors. It's easier for employees to follow established routines than it is for them to vary the routine according to each day's events. Take, for instance, a simple routine of sorting incoming mail before the end of each workday and placing it in the appropriate in-boxes. Once that routine is established, your secretary knows exactly what is expected, the mail ends up in the same place every day, and mail is rarely lost. If a temp is hired while the secretary goes on vacation, you can explain the mail system in a few sentences and feel secure that nothing will fall through the cracks.

Establishing a routine is equally important when several people work with shared information. A routine will increase the likelihood that data won't get lost or misfiled, and it will clarify the ground rules (for instance, no files get deleted unless the manager has signed off on them).

 Establishing routines will reduce tension. When you set up a routine for your staff to follow, you are responsible for it. If it works, wonderful. If there are problems, it's up to you to solve them. Either way, your employees know exactly what is expected of them and can try to meet those expectations. Routines prevent you from making vague demands that a task be done the right way. Unless you and your employees are on precisely the same wavelength, vague demands can damage both productivity and your staff's morale.

A routine that fits your needs increases productivity.

Getting Your Routines on Track

 Establishing routines will increase productivity. In the time you and your staff save by following established routines for the day-to-day running of your office, you can strategize for the future, solve problems, and in general get more work done.

 Establishing routines will improve everyone's learning curve and success rate. When a new system or piece of equipment is introduced at the workplace, establishing a routine for using it will help you and your staff maximize its benefits. Everyone will be in sync, will understand the system's quirks and shortcuts, and will be more likely to use it successfully from the beginning.

Be Flexible: Review and Revise

There's a difference between setting up workable routines and needlessly regimenting every procedure in your office. And even the most carefully thought-out routine can end up being off the mark, or too confusing, or simply not as efficient as you'd hoped it would be. So as your new office routine takes shape, regularly reassess the patterns and habits you've established. Ask your staff for their views as well.

Delivery Services

One routine worth cultivating is using the many delivery services now available. They can provide office products and lunchroom supplies, saving you or your staff shopping time. Less traditional delivery services such as dry cleaners don't relate specifically to business but cut down on the time you spend running mundane errands. Many cities have florists who will deliver a fresh arrangement to your office every week—a civilized touch that costs you no time at all.

Routines are fine for the daily tasks of running an office, but that is only part of the story. The tougher challenge is to know how to organize your time in any situation. The old adage, "If you need to get something done, get a busy person to do it," is true. Busy people have somehow learned the secrets of managing time effectively. You can too.

In the world of business there are six basic obstacles to organizing time:

- ❑ getting started in the morning
- ❑ planning your day
- ❑ procrastinating
- ❑ catching up with work you have put off
- ❑ succumbing to interruptions
- ❑ leaving work behind at the end of the day

Take a look at each obstacle in turn and see what you can do to overcome these time killers.

Getting Started in the Morning

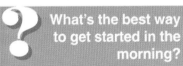
What's the best way to get started in the morning?

Simple: Set up an effective routine. You probably fall into some sort of routine naturally, but it may not be one that will help you get started. A certain buyer for a major department store got into the habit of drinking a cup of coffee every morning with two co-workers. It began as a brief exchange of pleasantries, but six months later it had become a forty-five-minute event. The bull session drained her and made it all the more difficult to settle down to work.

If you've fallen into a routine that hampers instead of helps you, it's time for a change. The first step in creating the optimum morning routine is taking a close, honest look at your past work habits. Review all the business situations you've experienced and determine which ones made you feel the most comfortable and productive. How were your mornings spent on those jobs? Could you re-create any of those elements now?

Next, assess the type of person you are and how it affects your work in the morning. Night owls may require two cups of strong espresso while listening to the news and rearranging the pen cup for twenty minutes. Morning people may want to plunge right in, checking messages, looking over yesterday's files, reviewing next week's calendar. It's best to acknowledge your natural inclinations as much as possible when designing your routine. Buck nature too much and you'll doom yourself to failure.

Clearly, your morning routine is going to reflect your specific tastes and needs. But taking that into account, try the tips on the following page.

Getting Started in the Morning

Eat breakfast at home, not at the office. If you work at home, leave the kitchen at a designated time each day and do not return, except to fetch a beverage if necessary, until morning break or lunchtime.

Make sure your routine includes something you will look forward to—a glass of fresh juice, a glance at *The Wall Street Journal,* watering the plants.

Exclude other people from your morning routine unless your business demands that you speak with vendors or clients first thing each day. This doesn't mean you must enter the office with eyes straight ahead, avoiding all casual conversation. Certainly you can chat with co-workers for a few moments. The morning routine often works best, however, if it is a solitary event. The purpose of the routine is to help you focus on the day ahead, and that takes concentration, not communication.

If possible, arrange not to be interrupted during your routine. Turn on the answering machine or have the receptionist take messages. Such isolation should last no longer than thirty minutes. If you just don't feel comfortable letting the phone ring, at least make the commitment to take work-related calls only—no gossip sessions or rambling analyses of last night's game.

**How can you
most effectively
plan your day?**

Planning the day's activities, whether done the evening before or as part of your morning routine, makes you *feel* organized. Better yet, you get a little zing of accomplishment before the day even begins. Many people never get around to planning the day because they're too frantic to catch up or too eager to confront the crisis left hanging from yesterday. That's a big mistake because planning the day automatically forces you to prioritize and to be proactive, not reactive. In the course of planning the day's activities, you might be surprised to discover that the crisis you were so tangled up in is actually less important than the client who'll come calling at 10:30.

The following steps are guaranteed to help you plan your day more productively.

Purchase a planner.
The planner is the single most important, yet inexpensive, way that you can stay on top of your daily activities. If you do nothing else about organizing your time, you must use a planner. There are many varieties of planners on the market, but they all contain essentially the same three

sections: calendars (daily, weekly, monthly) that let you record appointments and events, project pages, and expense pages.

You'll save yourself a lot of frustration and time by using a portable planner as opposed to a desktop planner. Portable planners are small enough to carry easily in a pocket, purse, or briefcase, and they save you from having to coordinate information from different calendars.

Your choice of planner will depend on the type of work you do and your particular organizational style. If you like to plan on a weekly basis, for example, choose one that lets you see your week at a glance. This type of planner is best for those who are usually called upon to schedule an appointment later in the week or month, rather than later in the day. Being able to see the entire week's activities enables you to make faster and better decisions about your time.

There are people, though, for whom daily planners make more sense than weekly planners. If your days are full of appointments and various scheduled activities, you may need enough space to schedule it all (and be able to read what you've written). Daily planners feature one page or a two-page spread for each day. Some include space for items such as a to-do list, appointments, phone calls, contacts, major projects, expenses, and so forth.

A weekly desk calendar helps you organize each day on paper.

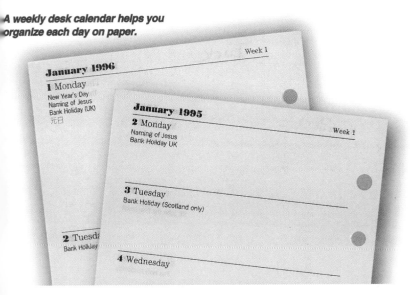

Planning Your Day

Make a list of the tasks that need to be accomplished. Find some time at the end of the workday or in the evening to jot down a to-do list (preferably in a daily planner) for the next day. At this point simply identify anything that needs to be done. You may then review this list as part of your morning routine the following day.

1 **Prioritize the tasks.** One common method of prioritizing tasks is to rank them from 1 to 10. But this method is time consuming if you're dealing with a lot of tasks, because it requires a considerable amount of thought as to the importance of each task. A less time-comsuming method is to judge tasks as A tasks and B tasks, with A tasks taking precedence over B tasks. Then look at the A list, choose the three most important tasks, and rank them 1, 2, 3. With this list you'll know where to begin your work in the morning. If you can complete those three tasks, you can go ahead and choose another three.

A Word to the Wise
Keep deadlines in mind when ranking tasks. Minor jobs that loiter at the bottom of the B list have a way of becoming crises if they're ignored for too long.

PLAN-A-MONTH®

	S	M	T	W	T	F	S	S	M	T	W	T	F	S	S	M	T	W	T	F	S
JAN							1	2	3	4	5	6	7	8	9	10	11	12	13	14	15
FEB		1	2	3	4	5	6	7	8	9	10	11	12	13	14	15	16	17	18	19	
MAR		1	2	3	4	5	6	7	8	9	10	11	12	13	14	15	16	17	18	19	
APR			1	2	3	4	5	6	7	8	9	10	11	12	13	14	15	16			
MAY	1	2	3	4	5	6	7	8	9	10	11	12	13	14	15	16	17	18	19	20	21
JUN			1	2	3	4	5	6	7	8	9	10	11	12	13	14	15	16	17	18	
JUL			1	2	3	4	5	6	7	8	9	10	11	12	13	14	15	16			
AUG	1	2	3	4	5	6	7	8	9	10	11	12	13	14	15	16	17	18	19	20	
SEP		1	2	3	4	5	6	7	8	9	10	11	12	13	14	15	16	17			
OCT			1	2	3	4	5	6	7	8	9	10	11	12	13	14	15				
NOV	1	2	3	4	5	6	7	8	9	10	11	12	13	14	15	16	17	18	19		
DEC		1	2	3	4	5	6	7	8	9	10	11	12	13	14	15	16	17			

To avoid procrastination, try the following techniques:

 Break the task or project down into smaller component tasks that are reasonably easy to achieve in a relatively short time. If a major project is facing you, it is often the anxiety over the magnitude of the work that prevents you from starting, and thereby completing, the project. Finishing the smaller component tasks will give you a sense of accomplishment that will help you move forward to complete the entire project.

 Do the task you don't want to do first. Often we avoid tasks not because they're so overwhelming, but because they're unpleasant. By getting these tasks out of the way early, you can avoid the tension and anticipation of facing them later. You may even find that the task really didn't take as long and wasn't as disagreeable as you thought it would be. Perhaps the best argument for dealing with tedious tasks first is that doing so clears your mind—and your schedule—for other tasks that are more enjoyable.

 Give yourself an incentive. You may get motivated to tackle the task if a reward is waiting for you when it's been completed. Telling yourself that when the task is done you can take a coffee break and read a few pages of a favorite book may be just what you need to get moving. You might even use a version of the incentive approach with your employees when they're facing a disagreeable task that has a tight deadline. Offering to order in lunch for everyone when the job is done might prove to be the motivator they need.

 Set deadlines for yourself and your employees. As long as deadlines don't send you into a panic, they can give you a reason to get started on something that you would otherwise put off as long as possible. This task is also true for your employees. Giving them a task without a due date encourages procrastination. Remember, they may not be as motivated to reach your goal as you are.

Overcoming Procrastination

There is a price for procrastination. For while you're catching up on overdue tasks, you must also cope with new tasks that need to be completed so you can meet your goals. The following steps will get you back on track, but in order for them to work you'll need to be diligent.

1. Make a list of all the tasks you have been avoiding. (Be honest.)

2. Rank them from most important to least important.

3. Now compare this list with the ordered list of activities you are currently working on.

4. Starting with the most important tasks on the catch-up list, resolve to do at least one task from this list, along with your current priority tasks, each day until you are caught up. If you complete one catch-up task, try to do another before the end of the day.

Lots of things can result in your work being interrupted. Phone calls, co-workers, and even your own lack of concentration can eat up valuable work time. A few organizing tactics will help you regain some of that lost time.

Define an off-limits period. Set aside a portion of the day during which you will not be interrupted by phone calls or co-workers except for emergencies. This off-limits period could be the time for you to work on one of those A list tasks you need to accomplish. To avoid problems, make sure that others in your office understand that during this time you are unavailable.

Close your office door. Often you're interrupted simply because someone walks by your door, sees you, and decides to stop in for some casual conversation or advice. Closing the door should signal to others that you are unavailable. Of course, there are always people who don't respect that signal. Therefore, let your co-workers and employees know in a friendly but firm way that you'll be happy to meet with them when your door is open—and not otherwise.

Post Your Availability

One CEO got so tired of employees knocking on her closed door and saying, "I'm sorry to bother you, but…" that she bought a small plastic clock sign of the type used by retail shops to post business hours. She tacked the sign to her door, set the clock's hands to the time she'd be available, and happily reported that it worked like a charm.

Limiting Interruptions

 Create imaginary barriers if necessary. If you don't have a private office, it's more difficult but not impossible. If you work in a cubicle or an open space, you have no physical barriers between you and others in the office, so you'll need to create imaginary barriers. Talk to your co-workers and let them know a regular time of the day when you'd like to work undisturbed (except for emergencies). If everyone else is also working in cubicles or open space, get together and develop a sign or signal that you all agree on—perhaps a small red three-by-five card that you can tack to the panel of your cubicle or place prominently on your desk. Then ask the reception-ist to hold your calls.

 Ask your secretary to run interference for you. Depending on the physical layout of the office, you may be able to situate your secretary's desk right outside your office so that employees and co-workers can be stopped from interrupting you.

 Have your answering machine or voice mail take messages for you. With voice-messaging equipment you don't have to be inter-rupted by phone calls—you can accept messages when you're ready for them. If there is someone (like a spouse or partner) whom you feel should have access to you at any time, you can designate one line on a multiline phone for that person.

Earplugs for Concentration

If you work in an open office or one with thin walls, try earplugs to cut down on distractions during your "off-limits" hours. New brands of earplugs are inexpen-sive, comfortable, and very effective.

It's 5:30, and you swear you'll leave the office after you put a few final touches on that proposal. Then suddenly it's 8:30, your angry spouse is on the phone, and the proposal is four pages longer but no closer to completion. Sound familiar?

For all working people, but particularly for those who own their own business, work can feel like a pit of quicksand—impossible to escape, sucking you back in just when you're about to reach for the door. People who work from home are especially susceptible to this, as their "home office" turns into an "office home" and finally into purgatory.

You *can* get away from your work, and indeed you need to on a regular oasis in order to clear your mind. Working constantly with no mental or physical rest can set up a never-ending cycle of exhaustion, incomplete projects, and anxiety. Without time away from the job, you can't get perspective on it, and perspective is crucial to making wise decisions.

Unless you're in the middle of a crisis, you should be able to arrange your business so that you can close up shop at a reasonable time each day. The following strategies will help you do it.

 Go home on time every day. Set up a work schedule, stick to it, and make sure your employees do too. Walk out the door and lock it behind you (unless your business requires shifts). Make no exceptions except for emergencies.

If this suggestion sounds too simple or impossible or outrageous, you need to take a hard look at your goals and expectations. Businesses that require endless hours of overtime are usually in the start-up phase, in crisis, or understaffed. The first two are temporary situations, although starting a business may require you to work long hours for many months. Understaffing, however, has become more prevalent in the last five or ten years as companies have tightened their belts by laying off workers and asking those who remain to work longer hours.

If your business is already established and it's still the norm for you or your employees to put in fifty- or sixty-hour weeks, think carefully about your priorities. Is this really how you want to spend your time indefinitely? Are your goals realistic? Or should you make some changes that would scale things back to a manageable level?

Planning Free Time

 Schedule free zones into your week if you work unusual hours. Consultants, sales representatives, and small-business owners often have the luxury of setting flexible work hours. But if your job does not require a nine-to-five schedule, you're actually *more* likely to put in extra hours. Because you can work at any time, the lines between business and leisure become blurred. Scheduling a free zone is particularly important for you. This free zone may be an afternoon one day, an evening on another. In addition, be sure to find at least one complete day every week during which you do no work for your business at all (for your sanity and health, two days would be better).

 Put upcoming social events on your calendar in the same way you record your business appointments. Social occasions are important for your well-being and a good excuse to get you away from work. But beware: some social occasions are actually business meetings in disguise—your professional organization's monthly dinner, a lunch date that's really a networking fest. Be sure to count such occasions as business, not recreational time, because you will inevitably spend the entire time talking business. Look for real social events for the diversion you need.

 Sign up for an exercise class that meets at least a couple of times a week and schedule it into your calendar. The class will get you away from work and force you to do something healthy. And you receive a side benefit: regular exercise gives you more stamina to do your work!

The ultimate time-management tool is delegation. It frees you up to do more pressing business and builds employees' self-reliance.

What is delegation?

Would you like an extra hour or two in each day, or an extra pair of hands? There is a magic wand you can wave to multiply the time you have to get things done. That magic wand is called delegation.

Simply stated, delegation is the assignment of a task to someone else, and there is no faster way to multiply the time you apply to a task than to delegate all or part of it. Typically, managers delegate to subordinates, but non-managers can delegate, too.

What happens if you don't delegate?

In addition to making you less effective, failing to delegate tasks deprives the people who work for you of the chance to develop the new skills and self-confidence they will need to continue to grow within the company. This handicaps the entire business. The whole organization becomes tentative, slow, and unresponsive, unable to quickly adapt to changes in work load or take advantage of business opportunities that arise.

What are the steps to effective delegation?

You can learn to delegate work by following these tried-and-true steps.

Let go. For many people this is easier said than done. Such people cling desperately to the old adage that says, "If you want something done right, do it yourself." Doing everything yourself automatically limits your success. At some point your business will exceed your physical capacity and will level off, or you will likely push yourself until your health deteriorates.

Accept all the right ways. If you find it hard to let go, you probably find it easy to jump back in when the person to whom you delegated the task doesn't do it the way you would have or as well. But it's probably good enough, and while that task was being done you were doing something else, thus effectively multiplying your time, which is the ultimate time-management technique.

Delegating

Assign the responsibility *and* the authority. It's possible to assign a task and have the person it is assigned to check back with you at every decision point. But if your goal is to multiply your own time, this may not be the best approach. It is far more desirable to delegate the task and the authority, and then hold the person receiving the task accountable for the outcome. This allows the individual to test his or her own capabilities while at the same time freeing you to tackle tasks that cannot be delegated.

Provide resources. Imagine being asked to wash the windows of a two-story building, but not being given a ladder. Don't do that when you delegate. Be sure to provide the resources, tools, training, and time needed to effectively complete the job.

Review progress. Without falling prey to the problems described above, take time to review the tasks you have delegated to others. Are they on schedule? Have any unexpected obstacles arisen? The review step is particularly important when dealing with the complexities inherent in major projects.

Managers Must Delegate

If you are a manager, never do anything someone else can do for you. There are tasks the owner of a business can do that no one else in the organization can—for example, arrange for additional capital investment or establish the firm's strategic direction. If you are spending your time doing things others could be doing for you, who will do the things only you can do?

❓ How can non-managers delegate?

People delegate laterally all the time. It usually starts like this: "Joe, can you do me a favor?" Asking a co-worker for help is another way of delegating. And it makes sense for everyone. If you're in the thick of it, why not ask a friend to lend a hand? Then, when you're caught up and your friend is swamped, you can reciprocate.

Non-managers can not only delegate laterally, they can also delegate upward. Yes, you can actually delegate tasks to your boss. It might go something like this: "I'm trying to get the budgets done by the end of the week, but I'm having trouble getting the figures from marketing and R&D. At this rate it'll take me forever. Maybe if you gave them a call and asked them to give you their numbers personally...?"

By delegating such a task to your boss you not only use your time more efficiently but also ensure your boss's goal will be achieved on time—both of which are beneficial to you.

5 Solving Problems Quickly

It would be glorious if by following all the advice in the previous chapter you could be master of the clock, entirely in control of your business. There's just one glitch: problems.

Problems are the black holes of business management. They inhale hours and hours of precious time, robbing you of the opportunity to really get things done, while sapping your strength, energy, and enthusiasm.

Unfortunately, there is no secret potion that will dissolve the myriad problems inherent in any business. However, there are some simple techniques that can help you solve your problems in less time, leaving you extra hours to devote to more productive endeavors.

? What causes problems?

All problems break down into two general categories: task-oriented problems and people-oriented problems. Problems involving people can be far more time consuming and emotionally draining than task-oriented problems.

Many books have been written about managing people, and we don't attempt to cover the topic in depth in this chapter. Instead, we present a distillation of basic, proven techniques for dealing with others effectively and efficiently. Learning and practicing these methods will save you hours of wasted effort and pointless squabbling.

Solving Task Problems

After outlining the techniques for dealing with task- and people-oriented problems, we'll take a look at some of the most common time wasters in business, and we'll suggest ways you can overcome them.

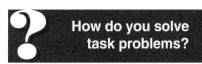

How do you solve task problems?

Complex tasks often present complex problems. Those problems translate into wasted time, which means overtime pay, missed deadlines, and a welter of other disasters. Here it's especially vital to understand the most time-efficient way of solving the problem.

First, ask yourself and your staff *where* the problem is:

❐ Where in the business? (sales, manufacturing, R&D?)

❐ Where in the operation? (initial assembly, testing?)

❐ Where geographically? (Which state, region, district?)

❐ Where in terms of people? (Who is and isn't involved?)

Next, ask *when* the problem occurs:

❐ What season, quarter, month, day, or time of day?

❐ When in the cycle? Does it occur regularly or randomly?

Learn to solve problems quickly, effectively, and efficiently.

Solving Task Problems

Next, follow these steps to home in on the exact nature of the problem.

 Note the differences. What is different about where the problem *does* exist versus where it does not, but logically should? For example, if the problem exists in the east and midwest region, why doesn't it exist in the south or west? If ten people perform the same task, why do only three experience the problem?

 Look for changes. If an operation has been running smoothly, then develops a problem, something must have changed. Has a new person been hired, a new process or procedure been introduced, or a new supplier been selected? Has an old machine gone out of alignment?

 Brainstorm possible causes. Assess the differences and the changes that have taken place and list all the possible causes you can think of. For particularly complex problems, it may help to organize the factors into the four M's: materials, methods, men, and machines.

 Select the most likely cause and test it. Select one of the possible causes and devise a plan to fix it. Next, implement your corrective action. Then evaluate the results. If the problem goes away, you nailed it with the first shot. If the problem is affected, try the other possible causes until you find the true cause of the problem.

Solving People Problems

? How do you solve people problems?

Knowing how to solve people problems quickly is crucial to your overall time-management scheme. Even if you're self-employed and have no staff, you work with others every day—vendors, clients, freelancers, salespeople. Deadlines must be met, schedules followed, products shipped, and all of it depends on people working together smoothly and swiftly.

Often, our first reaction to someone who fails to do what we've asked, whether it's an employee or a sales rep, is to threaten the person: "You'd better shape up or you're out of here!" or "Get that replacement part to me by Tuesday or your supervisor's gonna get an earful!" This tactic is unpleasant and often has only limited success. Fortunately, there is a better way.

Your first move must be to **define the problem.** Define it in terms of the difference between *should* and *actual*.

For example, John should be at work at 8:00, but actually arrives at 8:30.

Next you must **communicate the situation.** To communicate a problem to someone so that your message is understood and accepted, you need to be direct, specific, and nonpunishing. Don't beat around the bush. Don't be vague, and don't be sarcastic or threatening in word or tone of voice.

After you've stated the situation, listen carefully to what the other person has to say. You need to **determine the nature of the problem in terms of *can't* or *won't.*** Is John telling you that he can't arrive to work at 8:00, or that he won't do it? To distinguish between the two, ask yourself this: If you offered John one million dollars, could he get to work on time? If the answer is yes, the problem is *motivational.* If the answer is no (perhaps John's child-care responsibilities make it impossible for him to get to work by 8:00), the problem rests in his *ability* to do what you want.

51

Solving People Problems

❓ How do you solve an ability problem?

If an employee or associate wants to do what you request but can't—not even for a million dollars—start by asking for ideas. What have they tried? What would they like to try? If this proves unsuccessful, brainstorm with the other person. List as many ideas as the two of you can think of. Then review the list, select the best idea, and give it a try.

As the business owner or manager, you must be the one who keeps your eye on the ball. Sometimes the other person simply can't achieve the task at hand, and when that becomes clear, you may need to involve other people or rethink the project. From a time-management standpoint, it's essential that you learn to recognize (and act on) an impasse such as this. Only you can determine how much time you want to spend training someone or experimenting with different approaches

❓ How do you solve a motivational problem?

People are motivated by the consequences of their actions. In business situations, three types of consequences come into play:

❑ Consequences to specific tasks

❑ Consequences to other people

❑ Assigned consequences—that is, consequences that you, the boss or client or customer, determine and enforce

Solving People Problems

Motivational problems are solved by citing one of these consequences. In the case of a tardy employee, you may tell him that his work has been suffering because he's always rushing to make up for lost time. Or if he's the type of person who is more concerned about feelings and relationships than he is about tasks, remind him that his co-workers must cover for him when he's late. In many cases one of these approaches will be enough to straighten out the situation.

More often than we'd like, however, the only method that will work is the third one, assigning consequences. This is probably the technique your mother used at the dinner table ("Eat your peas, or no dessert.") It's not a pleasant experience for either party, and that's why it should be used as a last resort.

The consequences you assign depend, of course, on your position in the relationship.

❏ If you are the boss, the ultimate assigned consequence is that the employee will lose his or her job.

❏ If you are a client or customer, you can take your business elsewhere.

❏ If your problem is with someone who is paying for your services, you must decide when the frustration of dealing with the other party outweighs the financial benefits. You must, in other words, draw your line in the sand.

No matter what your position, you should carefully weigh your assigned consequences before verbalizing them. Remember the cardinal rule: Follow through on your assigned consequences! If you don't, your credibility is ruined and all the problem-solving techniques in the world won't help you then.

Resolving problems with people is a necessary part of doing business.

Tackling Common Time Wasters

The processes just outlined give you tools with which to tackle most business problems. But certain logjams seem to occur with grueling regularity in nearly every business. Here are some of the frequently encountered time-related problems, along with suggestions to help you resolve them quickly.

? Why can't your department meet deadlines?

Deadlines are largely determined by the promises made by salespeople who are measured by and rewarded for getting sales. Employees who produce goods are measured by and rewarded for making quality products, minimizing expenses, and keeping excess inventory low. The two sets of goals are often at cross-purposes, which results in the salespeople feeling pressured to keep the revenue flowing in and the manufacturing people feeling pressured by everything else—especially time.

Finding a solution is the responsibility of the person in the company who is equally concerned with the operation of both groups. In large companies, this person may be the general manager or someone who reports to him or her. In smaller companies, it may be the president.

This person's task is twofold. First, he or she must set ground rules that both sales and manufacturing can live with. Each side will need to compromise, and the person setting the rules must stand by them—or, if a juicy sales opportunity arises that just can't be turned down, the manager must be willing to hire additional help so deadlines can be met. Part of managing time effectively involves recognizing when the manpower-to-hour ratio simply isn't working.

The manager's second task is to look carefully at the personalities involved and determine whether a motivational problem is tainting the waters. If it is, the guidelines mentioned earlier should be helpful.

? Why does the staff walk around so much?

This could be a motivational problem, but often other factors are involved:

❒ Poorly planned traffic patterns cause a lot of extra footwork. It may be worth your while to reevaluate your office layout, and perhaps to hire a space planner. Bad traffic patterns also mean that employees are more likely to walk past co-workers and be tempted to shoot the breeze for a moment or two.

❒ A large percentage of the people in motion are probably on their way to and from the copier. Leasing a few small copy machines and placing them throughout the office may help. The same problem can occur with computer printers. In this instance, you might want to purchase several inexpensive printers to alleviate the gridlock, keeping your high-quality printer available for those who need top-notch print resolution.

Watch the Light

One company took an idea from the airlines when it installed a light above the copier that could be seen by the entire office. When the light was on, people knew the equipment was in use and could avoid an unnecessary walk.

? How can you rein in long breaks?

This is clearly a motivational problem, and one that should be handled firmly and consistently. You can cite consequences to the task: "Your work is getting sloppy because you're rushing it." Or you can cite consequences to other workers: "Susan has to keep covering for you when you're not there to take your calls."

Tackling Common Time Wasters

Keep in mind, however, that lunch hours and breaks reflect the corporate culture. This is particularly true in small and mid-sized organizations where most of the workers are aware of what management is doing. If you stick to the same schedule you expect of your staff, you'll find it a lot easier to state your case.

? Why are your vendor's shipments always late?

If you've thought it once, you've thought it a thousand times: "Am I the only person who cares about making a living? Don't these people need my business?" They may, and they may not. Perhaps their own time-management systems are in such disarray that they can't meet *any* of their clients' deadlines.

The solution to this problem is straightforward: assign consequences. The consequences don't have to be negative; you can offer incentives, such as paying within 15 days if the vendor is early. This is sometimes the best way to go if you're satisfied with everything except their tardiness, or if you don't have time to look for someone new, or if there is no other similar vendor to whom you can turn.

If the town is full of vendors offering similar services, you have more choices. You can impose late charges, or award half your business to another vendor, or tell them that if they don't start meeting your deadlines you'll have to stop using them entirely. But be careful how you approach this—have a backup in place before you issue your warning. They might assume they're losing your business no matter what, and service could get even worse, so be prepared.

The processes outlined in this chapter will save you time by organizing your problem-solving efforts. They are particularly useful in an office setting but are also invaluable to consultants and small-business people who work out of their homes—a work force that is growing by leaps and bounds. Those who make their home their office face special challenges when it comes to managing time. In the next chapter we'll offer some key advice on how to deal with the temptations and obstacles inherent in the home-office setting.

Organizing Your Home Office

6

f commercial workplaces need organizational systems to be more efficient, home-based businesses need them to survive. Away from the formal structure of a commercial office and tempted by the pleasures and daily demands of a home environment, the home-based business owner needs organization and routines as incentives just to go to work each day.

? What is the advantage of working from home?

There is a big plus to working from home, however. Home-based business owners and telecommuters (those who spend at least part of their week working from home via computers and fax machines) have the freedom to create a work environment that fits their personality and preferences. If the nine-to-five routine never suited you because you're a late-night person, you may decide to begin work at 5:00 P.M. and work into the wee hours of the morning. Or you can work mornings and evenings, leaving the afternoon free to run errands. You determine your schedule.

If you work at home, you should set aside a specific work area, preferably in a room that is not used as living space during the hours you'll be working. Ideally this room should have a door to close yourself off from your domestic life. By physically separating yourself from the rest of the family, you emphasize your identity as a working person and decrease the likelihood of interruptions.

Establishing Parameters

? Why organize at home?

Most people who work from home would admit that self-motivation is one of their biggest challenges. Organization and routines can be invaluable aids here, helping you to conquer procrastination and avoidance of work. Self-motivation is a complex psychological issue, but there's no doubt that the more smoothly your office runs, the more likely you are to feel in control of your work. That alone is a motivating factor.

To get organized, home-based workers must first focus on the parameters of their business. The following questions will help you determine yours. It's a good idea to write down your answers so that you can easily review them.

Create boundaries for your home office.

? How many days of the week do you want to work?

Remember, you don't have to work five days a week just because it seems that everyone else is. *You* have control. If you can do the work for your business in three or four days, that's all you need to work. Naturally, a big factor in this decision is how much money you want to make.

? How many hours a day should you work?

To figure this out, turn back to your goals. How long will each take? What are your deadlines? Only you can determine how many hours it will take to complete the work. If you figure that a task will take five hours to complete, you can choose to do it in one sitting or at a leisurely pace of an hour a day.

Establishing Parameters

Which hours do you want to work?

Choose times that are appropriate for your type of business as well as your work style and personal needs. If clients expect to be able to reach you during regular business hours, you'll probably want to be available to take calls. If you absolutely don't want to work normal business hours, let your clients know the hours you will be available.

Many home-based consultants charge clients a per-hour fee. The best way to keep track of your hours is to buy an inexpensive stopwatch at a sporting goods store, set it to zero at the beginning of each workday, and record the total minutes at the end of the day. If you're interrupted during the day, simply stop the clock until you can resume work.

When will you take breaks?

Some people like to break at the same time each day; others feel that being flexible about their breaks is one of the joys of working from home. Either choice is fine. The important thing is to set a time limit on lunch and breaks. Most people allow an hour for lunch and one fifteen- or twenty-minute break in the morning and afternoon.

Although you must limit the amount of time you spend on breaks, it's equally important not to skip them. When you're working at home, hours can pass while you sit staring at a screen or talking on the phone. Getting up to stretch and eat a healthy snack or meal keeps you from getting bleary or burned out.

Coffee Time
A freelance designer and coffee addict decided to see how much time she spent in the kitchen grinding and brewing her beloved java. She was shocked to discover that she lost nearly an hour to this ritual every day. Her solution: She bought a small coffee maker and put it in her office. She now grinds the beans before she starts work and when she makes her coffee, it takes just a minute to pour the grounds and turn on the machine. Then she works until her next cup is ready.

Do your work and personal schedules mesh?

Be sure to consider the effect personal responsibilities (children, spouse, parents, and so forth) will have on your business hours. If you're a working parent, for example, you'll certainly need to schedule your work hours around those times when your children are either in school or with a sitter. But examine less obvious elements too—your children's extracurricular activities, taking clothes to the cleaners, shopping for groceries. If you write them down, you'll get an idea of just how much time these errands consume. Planning wisely, you may be able to combine everything into one or two blocks of time during the week, which will give you more time to work and fewer excuses to avoid working.

Balancing Work and Family

How will you set boundaries?

One of the most difficult aspects of working from home is convincing the family that your business or work really is a job, just like any other. Unless you establish clear times when you are unavailable except for emergencies, you may find that you're continually drawn away from business by your family's inconsequential demands. Several steps are helpful when hammering out the work-versus-family issue.

 Discuss with your family why you are working and when you will work. Set up a work schedule with office hours and tell your family when you will be available. Stress the importance of your home office and let them know that you are working at home just the same as you would in a company office.

 Set up a regular work schedule and post it on the door of the room where you work. Stick to the schedule, and that includes quitting time: If you tell your family you'll turn off the computer at 4:30, do it.

 Establish parameters: "Don't knock on my door unless someone is hurt or a stranger is at the door." Enforce these parameters. If you don't, they'll quickly fall by the wayside.

 Don't let guilt about not being constantly available to your family undermine your business efforts. Chances are your work isn't just a hobby—you need the money. It's therefore probably more to your family's benefit that you have uninterrupted work time than that you settle every argument or respond to every demand.

What will you do with the kids?

Parents who work at home are nearly unanimous about one point: If you have young children you'll need to arrange for child care so you have sufficient periods of uninterrupted time to complete your work on schedule. Otherwise you'll be hassled constantly and will never accomplish anything.

Keeping Your Office Businesslike

❓ How can you deflect interruptions?

In addition to family demands, you may find yourself interrupted by a variety of different people: salespeople, friends, neighbors, and so forth. Rather than making judgment calls at the moment or slamming doors on people and offending them, establish a policy that lets you treat them all fairly. Don't be afraid to announce to friends and neighbors that during certain hours of the day you will be at work and un-available. And don't be afraid to ignore the doorbell if it isn't convenient. If it's an emergency, you'll know it.

If you work at a job that requires quiet time during the day, look into an electronic phone system that sends calls directly to voice mail when you're not available. Without these interruptions, you'll increase your productivity and be more receptive when you are taking calls.

"I'm on a Deadline"

One journalist's magical formula for cutting interruptions short is to simply utter the sentence, "I'm on a deadline." No one can take offense at that, and it gets you out of the conversation instantly. Try it—the results will amaze you.

Keep your home office professional.

❓ How will you handle household chores?

If you can't afford to have a house-keeper once or twice during the week, you'll need to schedule time to do household chores. You may want to use these chores as a break from work, or you may choose to start or end the day with them. The problem with starting the day with household tasks, however, is that you can end up putting off work for the entire day. Organize household tasks in the same manner as business tasks: prioritize them and plan for them on your calendar.

Now that you've answered these questions, you should have a clearer concept of the way your typical work-day will flow. With that in mind, move on to the next step as discussed in chapter 7: organizing the mountain of paperwork you've been avoiding all this time.

A Word to the Wise

If you see clients in your home office, try to keep it tidy. That goes, too, for the route through your house that leads to your office. A commercial office that's unclean and strewn with overflowing boxes and stacks of paper might make a client nervous, and your home office is no different.

Organizing Paper

The first chapter of this book mentioned the myth of the paperless office. No doubt you can personally attest to the fact that paper is still very much a part of business. And paper may well be the bane of your existence—so much paper may come your way every day that you can barely clear the room you need on your desk to write more things down on paper!

Don't expect the situation to change anytime soon. Even if you vow to create a totally paperless office by generating and storing files only on computer, you still have to deal with the outside world. The Association for Information and Image Management estimates that only about 4 percent of all documents are in electronic form. There's no way around it, then: You need paper filing systems for much of what you do and storage cabinets,

office space, and—depending on the size of your business—personnel to file and retrieve documents. If your business requires that you retain files for several years (for example, IRS tax forms and supporting material), you may even need to rent storage space for your paper tiger.

 ## What is meant by paper?

It's not just reports neatly typed on 8 1/2" x 11" sheets. The paper you work with every day is literally anything in print form: reports, brochures, catalogs, articles, and on and on. This welter of data is located on that remarkable paper magnet—your desk.

Basic Tools of Organization

Most people try to organize their desks or work spaces so that everything they need is an arm's length away. The following organizational aids are considered to be the basic "tool kit" for efficient daily operations.

☐ **Active files.** Active files are those that you are currently working on. They can be placed in a hanging-file rack on the desk or in stacking baskets. A hanging-file rack is much like a mini-file drawer with the files ordered alphabetically. If your desk contains a file drawer (most do), you can also use that for your active files.

☐ **To-do list.** Somewhere on your desk or pegged to the wall of your workstation you should have a list of the tasks to be accomplished that day. Remember, you should have created that list at the end of the previous day.

☐ **Calendar.** A calendar holds a record of important events and appointments. This calendar may be large, with boxes for each day, or small and portable like a daily planner. Another alternative is to use an electronic organizer that accomplishes the same functions as a daily planner with the additional benefit of containing an address book (more on these in chapter 9).

☐ **In-box.** An in-box is a place to park paper, mail, and files until you have time to sort them.

☐ **Rolodex.** With a Rolodex or rotary file, you can keep telephone numbers and addresses handy and organized alphabetically.

☐ **Recycling bin.** This is a nineties term for the wastepaper basket. Environmentally friendly businesses recycle their paper; some even use different-colored bins to separate white paper from colored paper or paper trash from other waste.

☐ **Computer.** The most important paper organizer and filing system is the computer. It can replace many of the items above. We'll discuss the role of the computer in your efforts to manage information in chapter 9.

Each of these items has a role to play in managing the paper in your office, but the most vital tool for organzing paper is the one we will discuss next: the filing system.

Filing Systems

How do you set up a filing system?

If you've been in business any time at all, you already have a filing system. At least, you have cabinets stuffed with files, which may even be in alphabetical order. Filing systems are at the very heart of office organization, but few business owners understand how to set them up for greatest efficiency. Consequently, although most of your paper may be in files, there may in fact be no *system*—which is why your information is so unmanageable.

Don't despair. The following pages will reveal all you need to transform your filing system. The principles that you'll learn for paper filing systems also hold true for computer filing systems.

What are filing conventions?

Filing conventions are simply a set of rules for filing documents in your business. With a set of written filing conventions understood by everyone in the office, documents are less likely to be misfiled or lost.

Most businesses, however, have a human filing convention—that is, one person who controls and understands the filing system. The scene usually goes something like this: You hire someone to manage the clerical aspects of your business, and he develops a filing system. On his desk sits a "to-be-filed" basket, into which other employees place documents so that he may file them correctly. It works like

magic until the day this individual leaves to take another job. With him go the filing conventions he created and stored in his head. Now no one knows how anything is filed.

What is the solution?

Creating permanent filing conventions is the only way to avoid this problem. The owner and key employees agree on a system that is appropriate for the business, put it in writing, and train new people to use it. That way no *one* person has the power to throw the entire business into crisis.

What types of files are used?

Two types of files are used most frequently: file folders and hanging files. The file folder is the tabbed file that holds documents; the hanging file is what the file folder goes into. Hanging files are folders with brackets at the edges for easy gliding along a metal frame that fits inside a standard filing cabinet (although most cabinets are now designed to accommodate hanging files without the frame).

Technically, you don't need hanging files for items that only require a single file folder. But, in reality, business dealings are often too complex for a single file. Files that begin with a letter or two have a way of expanding, and when they do, you'll need to create a hanging file for the second-level material. File drawers cannot support both types at once—the file folders will slip down between the hanging files. So you need to make a decision about which type of file you'll use. You should employ hanging files unless you're absolutely certain that the information you're dealing with will remain very compact. For files that are bound to be really large, such as the chronological files mentioned in the next section, you'll want to purchase accordian-style folders.

 What categories of files will you have?

Before you set up your filing conventions, consider the various categories of files the typical business requires.

❐ **Client or customer files.** Whether you provide a product or a service, you'll be dealing with clients and customers and will want to maintain information on them.

❐ **Subject files.** Subject files contain information on various topics that may be of interest to the business, such as computer hardware or government grants.

❐ **Project files.** Whenever you're working on a specific project—for example, developing a site for a retail center—you'll want to create a file to contain all the information you gather on the topic.

❐ **Chronological files.** These files are simply a way to organize information daily, monthly, or yearly. They can contain copies of correspondence, statements, invoices, or payments.

❐ **Tickler files.** These chronological files remind you of things you'll need to do at some future date—attend a conference, pay a vendor, submit a bid, and so forth.

❐ **Miscellaneous correspondence files.** If you tend to send out or receive a lot of miscellaneous correspondence, you can create a file that contains these letters in the order of date sent or received, with the most recent at the front of the file. This is a good practice for filing short-term correspondence as well, if you'll only be sending out two or three items. Should a correspondent become a regular client or customer, you can start a separate client file for him or her.

First-Level Filing Conventions

First-level filing conventions consist of filing alphabetically or by number. Here is how each type of file discussed on the previous page is handled using a first-level filing convention.

 Client or customer files. These files are usually ordered alphabetically by the last name of the client or the company name. While alphabetical filing is probably the most common method, businesses with many clients, such as physicians, often use a numerical system, assigning each client an identifying number. This way, they don't have the problem of deciding how to handle three Joe Browns or two Susan Smiths. When dealing with more than one person from a company, you will want to index the file by the company name (such as Mosaic Clothing Co.). Within that major heading, you will arrange files alphabetically by the individuals' last names.

 Subject files. When you file subject files alphabetically, you must title the file with commonly used words, such as *government grants.* Use the first word that comes to mind when you are thinking about the subject. Keep a master list of the subject files and what they contain in case you forget what term you chose for a subject.

 Project files. When these files are ordered alphabetically, they can be titled generically based on the type of project (Feasibility Study: Moving the Office) or by the actual name of the project (Tuxedo Park Retail Center). Note that the wording of the first example suggests that Moving the Office is only one of several feasibility studies you are doing at the current time.

 Chronological files. Set up a file for each day of the month (1, 2, 3, 4, and so forth). Then, as correspondence, statements, invoices, or payments go out, place a copy in the file for the date the item was sent and a copy in the appropriate client, subject, or project file. At the end of the month, purge these files after making sure that you have a copy of each document in the appropriate main file. In this way you will know that you have a record of everything sent from your business during the present month, which is a lifesaver if for some reason you are unable to locate a document in the main file.

 Tickler files. These files are often organized by date. Set up files representing the twelve months of the year. As a piece of information comes into the office (for example, the announcement of an upcoming conference you want to attend), put it in the file for the month during which you should *respond* to the announcement. The tickler file is an excellent way of rerouting material from your in-box.

 Miscellaneous correspondence files. File correspondence that does not have a client, subject, or project file in your system in a single, chronologically ordered file folder with the most recent date on top. Periodically check this file to note if any of these miscellaneous documents from a particular source are frequent enough to warrant their own file. After six months or a year, you can feel safe in purging the documents in this file.

Second-Level Filing Conventions

First-level filing conventions are fairly straightforward, but your business dealings aren't always so simple. Consider the feasibility-study file previously discussed. What if you're doing more than one feasibility study? In that case you should have a second-level filing convention. Under the main category, Feasibility Studies, you can file each study alphabetically by its title:

Second-level filing conventions can take a number of different forms. Let's say you have a major client, Mosaic Clothing Company. If you're dealing with more than one person from the company, your hanging-file index tab should say Mosaic Clothing Co. Inside that hanging file, you'll place file folders labeled with the names of the Mosaic clients. These are filed alphabetically by the clients' last names:

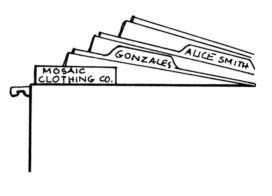

Perhaps you deal with departments within an organization. In that case you can organize your files using the company name as the hanging file and filing departments alphabetically within it:

Or maybe you own an advertising agency, and Mosaic has hired you to develop an ad campaign. In that case, you could file the various aspects and stages of the campaign within the hanging file. Again, you would file the internal folders alphabetically:

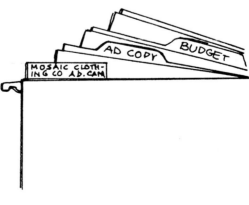

More Filing Conventions

Do third- and fourth-level filing conventions exist?

Theoretically, filing levels could go on indefinitely, but they're limited by the physical capacity of file folders. (This is not the case for computer filing systems, as discussed in chapter 9.) In most businesses, the third level of filing ends up being the filing cabinet drawer. These are generally labeled by category (Financial Reports) or by alphabetical order (A–D, E–H, and so forth). The method you choose depends on the type of business you have. It's a good idea to ask everyone who'll be dealing with the filing system which method they think will work best. If you're lucky, there will be a consensus about it. If not, you'll have to make a choice and proceed from there.

What's the best way to alphabetize?

You've probably noticed that alphabetizing is the key to filing. Alphabetizing is crucial to maintaining fast, universal access to filed information for everyone in the office. You must be as vigilant about it as was your high school English teacher. Within a single hanging file it's not disastrous if you're sloppy, although it can be annoying. However, within a drawer full of hanging files, sloppiness can be catastrophic.

You may want to spell out the basics of alphabetizing in your written filing conventions. Where problems usually arise is when there's a question about whether to alphabetize letter-by-letter or word-by-word. With the letter-by-letter method, spaces between words are ignored—the entire file title is treated as if it were one word. With the word-by-word method, files are alphabetized according to the first word, and beyond that are filed alphabetically according to the second word. Here's an example.

Letter-by-letter	Word-by-word
New clients	New clients
Newhall Co.	New York
News articles	Newhall Co.
New York	News articles

The letter-by-letter method is better because it's more straightforward and easier to explain.

Writing down the filing conventions

Once you've determined which method you'll use to organize your files, write it down in the simplest possible language. If your associate (or spouse or friend) is better with words than you are, let that person do it. Don't go overboard, outlining every possible filing scenario. Just state the facts. For example:

MOSAIC CLOTHING CO. Filing Conventions

1. We have four kinds of files: client files, project files, correspondence files, and a monthly chronological file.

2. Client, project, and correspondence files are organized alphabetically, letter-by-letter.

3. The chronological file is organized by day and is purged at the end of every month.

4. The file cabinet drawers are organized by category. Consult with the manager if you want to create a new one.

It's an enormous hassle to change a filing system once it's been established, so think carefully about the filing conventions you want to implement. If you have a secretary who is familiar with filing, enlist his or her aid in developing the system. Flexibility is an asset in many areas of business, but it's best to get your filing system right the first time.

Once you've set up your filing conventions and have the system in place, the following tips will help you keep things purring along.

✔ Always put a file folder back where it came from immediately after using it.

✔ To make it easier to find a file's correct location, leave the next file folder pulled up an inch or so to mark the spot.

✔ Put the most recent information in the front of the file.

✔ Label every file.

✔ Carefully label every storage box or cabinet in which you place files, especially if you won't be using the files very often.

✔ File information when you get it. Avoid creating piles of documents to be filed.

✔ If you make duplicate copies of things like letters, be sure to stamp the copy that belongs in the file <u>FILE COPY</u> so it is always returned to its file.

✔ As files get large, break them into sub-files to speed up access to the information in them.

✔ Staple papers together rather than using paper clips, which tend to come off or get stuck on the file folder or on other papers in the file.

✔ To ensure that individual papers don't get lost from a file, try using fastener-type folders. These are designed with two brads at the top; each sheet must be punched with holes for the brads to slip through. This procedure works best if you have someone assigned to file maintenance, because it's more time consuming than regular filing.

✔ Reduce legal-size documents to letter size on a copier so that you only need one type of filing cabinet. This tactic also makes it easier to move groups of files. If, however, you deal with a lot of legal-size documents, it's probably better to have a separate filing cabinet for them.

✔ Use colored file folders and hanging files to make it easier to find things. (They're also more cheery than olive-drab files.) For instance, you could use red folders for accounts payable and green for accounts receivable.

✔ Keep a list of your filing conventions and the titles of your main files so that everyone always knows how to file a particular document and can easily train new staff to do the same.

Business Cards

A smoothly operating filing system will make most of those overwhelming stacks of paper in your office disappear. But there are some errant paper problems that call for special paper-taming techniques.

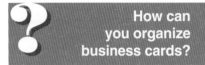

How can you organize business cards?

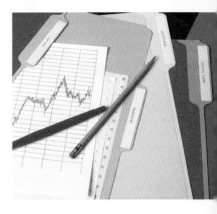

If you recoil when you hear the words "here's my card," it's probably because you already have a drawer full of business cards dating back to the paleolithic period. Of course, plenty of business cards never even make it to the drawer. Instead, they end up wadded in a back pocket or molding in a corner of your briefcase. That's a shame, because a well-organized collection of business cards is a valuable resource. There are several systems that work well for storing business cards.

A Rolodex or rotary filing system. Office-supply stores sell plastic jackets that fit onto rotary files and into which you can slip business cards. You can either maintain a separate rotary file for business cards or mix the business cards in with your regular rotary file. The only drawback to this system is that the information on the card is sometimes obscured because it falls

below the slots. If this occurs, just write that information on another part of the card.

Business card books. Like rotary files, these books have plastic jackets into which you insert business cards. They operate much like an address book and are indexed alphabetically.

File folders. Affix the business card to the inside of the appropriate file folder. This system works well when the information on the card is only needed at the time the file folder is being used, for example, for billing or correspondence.

Business card scanners. This state-of-the-art technology lets you input the information on your business card

without ever touching the computer keyboard. The card scanner is about the size of a Walkman and hooks into the parallel port of your computer. You insert the card and the information on it is read into the computer as text. It even recognizes fields such as name, address, and phone number. *Card Grabber* from Pacific Crest Technologies is one such card scanner.

The U.S. mail is probably the biggest conduit for information flowing into your office. You can let mail control you, or you can control it by following these three rules.

❒ **Open your mail as soon as you receive it.** The main problem with letting mail stack up is that, as the stack grows larger and larger, the task of sorting it becomes ever more daunting. Putting off opening your mail can cost you money too: You may miss an opportunity or fail to meet a deadline.

❒ **Designate a place in your office to sort and deal with mail.** Devote a corner of the main office (or a separate office space if you can spare it) to mailing and shipping. This space should include a counter for sorting, mail-message slots for employees, and supplies (scale, meter, stamps, envelopes). For top efficiency, place your copy machine, paper cutter, hole punch, and so forth in the same area.

❒ **Establish a rule that every piece of mail you receive will be acted on immediately, filed, or thrown out.** If you have a secretary, he or she can screen the mail for items you should review right away. Your secretary can also sort and file the rest of your mail and throw out the junk. But make sure you've defined *junk mail*—the catalog that looks like junk to your secretary may be one you've been waiting weeks to receive.

Stamps the Easy Way

The most efficient way to pay for outgoing mail is to use a postage meter. If you don't send enough mail to warrant one, ask your mail carrier about getting your stamps by mail. Some bank ATM machines are also conveniently selling stamps. No more waiting in line at the post office!

Taming the Mail

Whether you handle your own mail or someone else does, there are only five acceptable things to do with incoming mail:

1. Respond to it. If it's correspondence you're interested in, make a phone call or write back to the person to follow up on the subject at hand. You promptness will be appreciated, and you'll maintain your business at a higher level of activity.

2. Throw it in the recycling bin. Reading every piece of unsolicited junk mail is time consuming. If the piece of mail does not immediately interest you (the advertising usually starts on the envelope), get rid of it. If you set it aside to be examined later, you have only added to your work load.

3. Put it in the appropriate file. Information that you want to keep and read at your leisure—in other words, something that doesn't need to be acted on immediately—should be filed where you can easily find it.

❐ Put it in a subject file if it is information about a topic that interests you.

❐ Put it in a chronological file if it is information that you'll need at a later date.

❐ Put it in the appropriate client, subject, or project file if it doesn't need to be reviewed by anyone (for example, copies of already approved agreements).

4. Put it in the active file for accounts payable. Invoices and othe bills to be paid according to your normal billing cycle (see chapter 8, "Managing Money") should be temporarily stored in an active file. If you usually pay bills on the fifteenth and thirtieth of each month, you should set up two active file folders, one for each date. When an invoice comes in, place it in the file folder for the date it will be paid. That way when you or your bookkeeper sits down on the fifteenth of the month to pay the bills, all the bills that need to be paid will be in one place.

5. Transfer it to the appropriate person. Distribute all mail that goes to others immediately. Make file copies of important document (if they are not confidential) before sending them on to the appropriate person.

If you follow these five simple guidelines when opening the mail, you won't fall prey to the ugly, unmanageable stack of paper that looms over many people's desks. Quick, efficient delegation of the mail is the easiest way to reduce office clutter.

❓ What is the best way to route paper?

Dealing with mail inevitably results in needing to forward printed material to others. An efficient way to do this is via a routing slip. Easily made, these small slips of paper consist of two components: a section identifying the recipient and a section explaining why you're sending the material. Here's an example of a typical routing slip:

Attach a routing slip like this to a memo and check the name of the person you want to send it to, or write in the name if it's someone you do not normally send material to. Then check the appropriate action, and drop it in your out-basket or their in-basket.

If you check the names of several people, your secretary can make the necessary photocopies with the routing slip still attached, and then forward the material via the interoffice mail.

From: John Tesh

Route to:
- ❏ Mary Hart
- ❏ Leeza Gibbons
- ❏ Leonard Maltin
- ❏ Bob Goen

Action to be taken:
- ❏ FYI
- ❏ Please handle
- ❏ Let's discuss this

Date: _____

- ❏ _____
- ❏ _____
- ❏ _____
- ❏ _____

- ❏ Read & pass along
- ❏ Read & return
- ❏ Other:

Phone Messages

The key to handling telephone messages is to have the tools you need close at hand. You and your secretary, if you have one, will need the following.

 A message pad. A spiral-bound message book that makes carbon copies is best. That way you'll be creating a record of all messages received in case one gets lost. It also becomes a journal of the activities of your business. If you use an answering machine, transfer the messages to the book as you listen to them.

 A pen that won't walk away from the phone. Purchase a pen that attaches by a cord to your phone. This way you can be sure it will be there when you need it.

 Your Rolodex, business cards, or phone book. Business and networking go hand in hand. In case you want to refer a caller to someone else, have your resources close by.

Hands-Free Phoning

If you spend a lot of time on the telephone, it's probably worthwhile to invest in a headset. Headsets leave you free to take notes or access computer files, and without a doubt they're better for your neck and back than traditional handsets. You can buy a headset that connects to your existing phone or a portable one that allows you to roam your office at will.

Storing Other Media

Magazines, books, newsletters, audio cassettes, and video tapes are a vital part of this multimedia business age. Here's how to store them.

Magazines. Use plastic or cardboard storage racks to store the magazines in an upright position. These racks are available at office-supply stores and through mail-order catalogs. They should be labeled according to the name of the magazine or to the general subject covered by the magazine. You may want to include the date range on the label as well.

If you're ambitious, there's an even more efficient way to store information from magazines. The head chef at a major hotel said this technique increased her bank of usable information tenfold. She purchased large three-ring binders and boxes of clear plastic 8 1/2" x 11" sleeves, which come prepunched to fit in the binders. Once a month she'd sit down with the stack of magazines she'd received in the previous weeks and cut out the articles she wanted to save. She'd slip the article into the plastic jackets with the accompanying photographs highly visible. Tabbed divider sheets separated the binders into sections on recipes, preparation techniques, food trends, and so forth.

Audio and video tapes. Purchase special cabinets that have the appropriate-size slots and labeling materials to store your audio cassette and video tapes. Then use the filing conventions discussed earlier to organize the cabinets and their contents. For example, one video cabinet might contain cassettes of commercials you've produced to market your products. You'd label it *Product Commercials* and would file the video cassettes alphabetically by the product name and date.

Newsletters. File newsletters in three-ring binders and label the binders by date.

Seeking Out Storage Space

❏ *For your supply cabinet, visit the housewares department. Lazy Susans can be packed with supplies that are accessible with a spin of the tray. If your shelf is large you can use Lazy Susans that have two or three levels (they're made to hold spices). Rectangular spice racks also work well for keeping items within easy reach.*

❏ *Buy undershelf baskets to utilize wasted space.*

❏ *Don't let a corner stand empty. Home furnishing stores offer corner cabinets and shelves in a variety of styles.*

❏ *Bathrooms are perfect for storing items you don't use frequently. Again, home furnishing stores sell attractive cabinets that will give you the storage space without the clutter.*

❏ *Use your imagination. Jewelry boxes, tool boxes, tackle boxes, sewing baskets, and much more can all be put to use for storing small but essential items.*

What Can You Throw Away?

Are you one of those people who can't stand to throw anything away? That attitude will work if you're organized and have lots of places to store things, but even the most ardent packrats sometimes get the urge to purge. A few easy rules will help you determine what can be thrown away and what must be saved.

❑ Save all legal documents such as contracts, warranties, and insurance policies permanently in a safe, fireproof place—a safety deposit box in a bank or a safe in your office.

Save tax records for at least seven years after you have filed the forms. After filing the current year's tax returns, make it a practice to put the previous year's returns in a storage file. Then throw away the seven-year-old tax file. (Of course, if you have the space, it can be advantageous to keep all tax records permanently for a more complete picture of how you've done financially over the years.)

❑ Periodically, perhaps at tax time, go through your files and get rid of those you no longer need. You'll need to establish some criteria for this: files of employees who are no longer with you, outdated technological information, and so forth.

❑ Save any files related to work that you are presently doing. Do not throw these files away until you're certain the project is finished and there is no possiblility of legal or tax repercussions. Three years is a conservative length of time to store them.

❑ Keep permanently those files that contain information that can't be replaced or would be too expensive to re-create.

8 Managing Money

When most people dream of starting a business, making a lot of money figures prominently in the fantasy. Keeping track of the money, however, is usually *not* part of the dream. They'll be making brilliant deals, or selling a zillion patented self-inflating tires, or jetting to the Caribbean to catch the total eclipse of the sun. The bookkeeper will handle the details.

This aversion to bookkeeping can have dire consequences. Of all the information that flows through an office, financial matters are most able to dramatically affect the business—for better or for worse. Not knowing how much money you have, where it is, and when it must be used is like playing poker without looking at the cards. Consider these possibilities:

❐ It is April 1. You've finally gotten around to thinking about taxes, and you can't find any of the receipts you need. Maybe the shoebox wasn't such a good idea!

❐ You have incurred some unusual expenses this month and don't know whether you have the money to pay them. Then a check bounces—and you have your answer.

❐ The bill from your distributor looks strangely familiar—you could swear you've already paid it. But it'll take hours to locate the documentation to back up your claim.

The situations just described are common among businesses that haven't established procedures for managing financial information. If you're feeling ashamed because of your inadequate money management, you can take some comfort in knowing you're not alone. Just ask a bank officer—he'll give you an earful on the subject.

There are two basic aspects of financial management: organizing the flow of financial information through your office and creating an operating budget. This book deals only with information management; creating a budget requires expertise that extends beyond the scope of information organization. Rest assured, however, that it's difficult to stay within budget unless your financial information is well organized.

Laying Your System's Foundation

If you are a sole proprietor or work from your home, you must keep your business expenses separate from your personal expenses by employing separate bank accounts and records. That said, before you can set up a financial-management system, you must make several basic decisions.

Choose a fiscal year. A **fiscal year** is simply any twelve-month period you designate as such. It ends on the last day of the last month in this period. The importance of the fiscal year is that it determines when you will pay income tax on the profits of the business. Once you have chosen a fiscal year, you cannot change it without permission from the IRS.

Depending on the type of business you operate, you will probably want to choose your fiscal year based on your best quarter in terms of revenues, so that you end the year with sales trending upward. This tactic is used by many retail operations, which tend to use the calendar year as their fiscal year because Christmas is usually the best season for retailers.

Choose a cash or accrual basis of recording income and payments. With the cash method of recording, you record your income when it is received and your expenses when they are paid. This method is very easy to use. Many small businesses that don't maintain inventories use the cash method of accounting.

Laying Your System's Foundation

If, however, your business maintains an inventory that produces income, you are required by the IRS to use the accrual basis of accounting. With this method you record income when it is earned, even if you haven't yet been paid, and expenses when they are incurred, even if you haven't yet paid them. In reality, you are accounting for the right to receive a certain amount of income and the obligation to pay a certain debt.

 Choose a single-entry or double-entry system. There are two ways to enter financial information into your records. The **single-entry system** is the easiest and most familiar to people because it is the same system you use to record entries into your personal checkbook. That is why it is often used by very small businesses. Simply put, you record the daily inflow and outflow of income and expenses in a ledger. At the end of the month, you create a summary of the month's receipts and disbursements. While this system is easy, it has the inherent problem of not balancing itself because you can't check your entries against anything else.

A **double-entry system** is exactly what it says. You enter each income and expense item twice: once as a debit to one account and once as a credit to another account. Most growing businesses choose this method because you can tell immediately when your books don't balance. If you choose this system, you should ask your accountant to help you set it up.

Depending on the type of business you have, you will need to keep track of

❐ bills the business must pay

❐ invoices you send to people who owe you money

❐ bank accounts, including checking accounts that must be balanced regularly

❐ inventories of products you sell if you are a retailer, wholesaler, or manufacturer

❐ product sales records, again if you are a retailer, wholesaler, or manufacturer

❐ time and expense records, if you bill clients in this manner (as do lawyers, consultants, and so forth)

? How often should you track financial information?

Every day. There's no better way to stay on top of your business than keeping daily financial records. When you do, you'll catch errors sooner and avoid playing catch-up at the end of the month. For a growing business, daily record keeping is definitely facilitated by having a bookkeeper. If you don't have the luxury of a full-time bookkeeper, here are some general rules about record keeping that will help you maintain control of your finances.

? How do you keep daily records?

If you're using the cash method of accounting, you will enter income and expenses into a journal of receipts and disbursements. If you're using the accrual method, however (and this is most common), you will enter transactions into the appropriate journals. These enable you to see the amount of cash coming in daily. The journals most often used by businesses are the sales journal, cash-receipts journal, cash-disbursements journal, and purchases journal.

Record Keeping

If your business has daily sales (as do retail businesses), keep a daily summary of sales and cash receipts so that you can see your total daily sales and verify the total of your cash receipts.

If you don't have a retail business and your bookkeeper comes in, say, twice a week, it is probably adequate to have her or him update the daily records on the days she or he is in.

How do you keep weekly records?

The weekly record keeping you do will simplify your end-of-the-month calculations. There are several types of records that should be attended to.

❑ **Post to the ledger.** The journal entries that you or your bookkeeper have been recording daily should be posted to a ledger, which is a collection of all the accounts of a business—for example, cash accounts and accounts receivable. Posting to the ledger means posting your daily journal entries to their appropriate accounts.

❑ **Keep track of supplier bills** on a weekly basis (or use your chronological file to prompt you) so you can take advantage of discounts offered for early payment. Be sure that when you pay an invoice or bill, you mark it paid (with the date) and keep all the supporting documents together so that you don't mistakenly pay the same bill twice.

❑ **Age accounts.** It is important that you keep track of what people owe you. You can do this through a process called **aging,** which is simply categorizing a customer's or client's account by the length of time before the bill is due. You can set up a table with all your clients or customers listed down the left-hand side of the page. Then, across the top, denote columns for 30 days, 60 days, and so forth. For each client or customer, mark the appropriate column.

CLIENT	Date Billed	30 Days	60 Days	90 Days	120 Days
Zoot Suit Inc.	8/4		✔		
Lotuswear	8/22	✔			
Tewa Corp.	8/23	✔			
Cleaning Crew	8/25			✔	

❑ **Keep payroll records.** Stay on top of payroll information. Record how much to pay and how much to withhold for each employee. This information will be important in reporting taxes to the state and federal government.

❑ **Keep track of taxes.** Depending on the type of business you have, you may be responsible for payroll taxes, sales taxes, federal unemployment tax, and business income tax. Each of these taxes is paid at a different time. Keeping track of your tax liability on a weekly basis is a preventive measure to assure that you will have the money to pay them when they come due.

❑ **Keep miscellaneous records.** Other financial records you will want to keep on a weekly basis are:
• insurance payments
• maintenance bills
• inventory status
• office upkeep documentation

The monthly records you keep will give you a picture of how your business is doing month to month and will help you make decisions about your business's future. Monthly records consist of the following.

Cash-flow statement. For a business owner, there is probably no financial statement more important than the cash-flow statement because you pay your expenses with cash from the business, *not profits*. Your business cannot survive for very long without a positive cash flow. The **cash-flow statement** is simply a record of the cash that flowed into and out of your business during the month. When more flowed in than out, your cash flow is positive. If more cash flowed out than in, you have a negative cash flow. The cash-flow statement is the electrocardiogram that measures the heartbeat of your business. The figures on it will dictate what your next moves should be.

Income statement. The **income statement,** also called a profit-and-loss statement, compares revenues and expenses over a specific period of time to determine if the business has made a profit or incurred a loss. (*Profit* is the positive difference between revenues and expenses; *loss* is the negative difference between revenues and expenses.) The income statement begins with sales, for which you may not have received payment. In this way it differs from the cash-flow statement, which only reflects cash that has actually been deposited to the business's bank account. The income statement also includes non-cash entries such as depreciation, accounts receivable, and accounts payable.

The key difference between the income statement and the cash-flow statement is that you pay your business's taxes based on the income statement (which reflects your profit and loss), whereas you pay your bills from the cash you generate as reflected in the cash-flow statement.

The balance sheet. The **balance sheet** tells you the worth of your business at any given time. It is based on an accounting equation that assumes the business's assets are equal to the financial rights of the people who have an interest in the business: the owners (equity holders) and the creditors (liability holders). Therefore, the accounting equation looks like this:

assets = liabilities + capital

The items on the balance sheet are actually the balances from each of the ledger accounts.

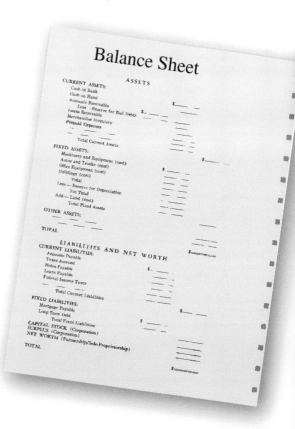

Putting Your System Together

How do you set up a financial-management system?

Hire an accountant. (If you already have one yet don't have any system, something is awry.) Whether you use an in-house accountant, an independent CPA, or one of the Big Six accounting firms, an accountant is an indispensable member of your business team. Your accountant will help you set up your books to ensure that you are doing them correctly, and the chart of accounts that he or she prepares will enable you to establish a filing system for financial records that corresponds to the categories on your financial statements, which will save the accountant time and you money at tax time.

Keep all your financial records and materials in one location for easy access, and designate a specific time to do all your financial record keeping. Depending on the type and size of the business, this time may be a certain hour of the day, a day of the week, twice a month—whatever it takes to stay on top of your records. The point is, be consistent.

Get the right record-keeping materials. Your accountant will tell you what kind of record-keeping supplies you'll need to buy. Any stationery supplier or office-supply store carries these financial systems, which include

- ❏ bookkeeping record books and ledgers
- ❏ payroll books to record wages, overtime pay, taxes and other withheld items
- ❏ inventory record books
- ❏ expense account diaries and vehicle mileage record books

Expense Account Diary and Vehicle Mileage Record

ELEMENTS REQUIRED BY LAW: (a) date; (b) item; (c) place; (d) business purpose; (e) name and business relationship of persons entertained; (f) amount

(a) DATE	(b) ITEM (c) PLACE (d) and (e)
3/8	Train fare - Prov. to New York and return
3/9	Breakfast - Deb's Coffee Shop, N.Y.C.
	Lunch with Mr. Doe of Doe Co. at Smith's
	Cocktails with Mr. Doe at Leone's
	Dinner at Mac's Steak House with Mr.
	Jones and 3 salesmen of XYZ Corp. -
	discussed several new products
	Taxi fares
	Phone calls
3/30	Breakfast - Deb's Coffee Shop
	Lunch - Beth's Diner
	Dinner with Mr. Hale of Hill Corp. at
	Beau Lingel restaurant - discussed
	promotion, advertising, etc.
3/31	Breakfast - Deb's Coffee Shop
	Taxi fares
	Lunch on train to Providence
	Hilton Hotel
	Postage
	Stationery

Optional	Miles — End of week	10424
Mileage	Miles — Beginning of week	10,239
Method	Miles traveled	135 at 27

Summary of Expenses

WEEK ENDING March 31,

ACCT. NO.	ACCOUNT	TOTAL THIS WEEK	TOTAL LAST WEEK	TOTAL TO DATE
1	BREAKFAST	10 60	66 75	77 35
2	LUNCH	28 05	118 30	146 35
3	DINNER	133 35	740 60	873 95
4	HOTEL OR MOTEL	150 00	900 00	1,050 00
5	TRANSPORTATION: PLANE			
6	RAILROAD	40 50	243 00	283 50
7	TAXI OR BUS	33 30	199 00	232 30
8	AUTO RENTAL, ETC.			
9	BAGGAGE CHARGES			
10	ENTERTAINMENT	11 60	181 50	193 10
11	GIFTS			
12	TIPS			
13	TELEPHONE	4 95	59 40	64 35
14	TOLLS			
15	POSTAGE	2 80	21 80	24 60
16	AUTO EXPENSE: GAS, OIL, LUBRICATION, ETC.			
17	REPAIRS			
18	TIRES, SUPPLIES, ETC.			
19	PARKING			
20	WASHING			
21	INSURANCE			
22	135 MILES @ 27.5¢	37 00	376 20	413 20
23	OFFICE EXPENSE	9 90	33 00	42 90
24	TRADE SHOWS			
25	MISCELLANEOUS			
26				
27				
28				
29				
30				
	TOTALS	462 05		

Computerizing Your Data

? What about computer accounting software?

You will save considerable time and effort converting at some point to a computerized accounting system, where one entry will place the information in several records at once. And there is another bonus: Fewer numbers to enter means fewer errors.

The type of computer accounting software you use will depend on the kind of business you have. The examples below refer to IBM PC software, but most or all of it is available for the Macintosh as well.

The small business. If your business has one or two people and you do not need to keep track of inventory, you can take advantage of a user-friendly and inexpensive software package such as *Quicken* by Intuit (under $50 as this is written). *Quicken* allows you to enter information as you would in a checkbook, reconcile the bank account, create budgets and reports, write and print checks, and pay bills electronically.

The service business. This type of business generates invoices and normally operates on a cash basis. A program like Intuit's *Quickbooks* may work for you. In addition to all the features of a program like *Quicken,* you can automatically bill customers with a new feature called "reimbursable-expense tracking." You can also file documents by month rather than by payee, which cuts down on elaborate filing mechanisms. And you can handle your payroll yourself. The Quickfill feature reduces data-entry time by recalling a previous entry for a client or supplier and filling it in for you. (The latest version of *Quicken* also has this feature.)

The growing business. As your business grows, you may need a more elaborate system to handle increased payroll, accounts receivable and payable, and other aspects of your business's finances. Consider a software package like *Peachtree Complete Accounting* or one of many other excellent programs. These programs normally have an on-screen tutorial and lots of help screens. Most give sample charts of accounts for different kinds of businesses, which reduces your set-up time. You can use the batch method where you save up the transactions to post all at once on certain dates or use the real-time method where transactions are recorded as they occur. The best programs also offer a choice of cash or accrual methods of accounting.

If your accounting program is designed for *Windows* as is *Peachtree for Windows,* you will be able to maintain several functions open at once on the screen, and each will be updated when you enter new information into one of them. For instance, you may post a transaction on a general expense ledger and the program will automatically update the ledger of the particular supplier you have posted.

Computerizing Your Data

? What about spreadsheets?

Spreadsheets offer yet another dimension of financial management. With spreadsheets you can prepare pro forma financial statements for forecasting, then manipulate the numbers to test various "what-if" scenarios.

For example, you might create a cash-flow statement and then vary sales depending on whether the economy is growing or stagnant as it relates to your business. As you change the numbers in the sales line, the computer will automatically change all the numbers affected by that new figure. Such forecasting will enable you to see the effect of a change in sales on all aspects of your business before it actually occurs. In fact, if you don't want to purchase an accounting software program, you can actually create the forms and accounts you need by using a spreadsheet. (It's wiser to get the accounting software, however. Who has time to reinvent the wheel?)

Don't Get Spreadsheet-Happy

Because spreadsheets make it so easy to deal with numbers in your business, there is a tendency to predict what should happen in your business based on the variables you project and to overlook what is happening. Don't get caught in limbo between projections and the reality of doing business. No matter how many fancy spreadsheets you create, the bottom line is, How much are you getting for your product or service, how much are you paying for it, and what's the difference between those two figures? Everything else is just support data.

? Do you need to keep paper records at all?

Yes. The Internal Revenue Service requires that you keep receipts and that you back up *on paper* all computer files that relate to taxes. Why? Because computer files can easily be tampered with.

The demands of the IRS are not the only reason that a paperless financial system is unrealistic at this time. Much of your business involves documents you receive from others—invoices, bills of sale, contracts, and so forth. Unless you're willing to scan all these documents into your computer for storage, you'll be storing them the old-fashioned way—in file folders.

How should you file paper records?

The types of files used for financial paperwork fall into the same general categories as those outlined in chapter 7.

❒ **Unpaid bills** can be filed in an alphabetized accordian file if you have a computer system that will track the due dates on these bill for you. If you don't have that software, a tickler file will serve the same purpose. Most people set up the tickler file so that bills are paid on the first and fifteenth of each month.

❒ **Bills you have paid** can best be documented by using voucher checks that come with two duplicate copies. The original gets sent to the payee. One copy goes into a file bearing the payee's name (which is organized alphabetically with other payee financial files). This copy also has any support data attached to it—documents such as vendor invoices, expense reports, or time reports. A second copy goes into a numerical file. No support data is attached to these checks—this file is purely for backup reference.

❒ **Invoices you've sent out** can be tracked by keeping two files, one for current invoices and one for those that are overdue. If your computer software does not provide an aging system for invoices, age them yourself by creating files for payments due in 30, 60, or 90 days (or however long you like).

Most financial software packages (which are discussed in chapter 9) will provide aging systems. In that case, you need only store the paper version of the invoice in an accounts receivable file that is ordered chronologically. Companies that generate many invoices every month often file them by invoice number instead of by date.

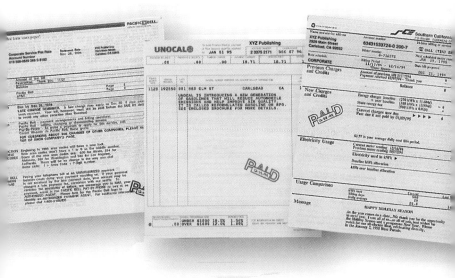

Filing Financial Records

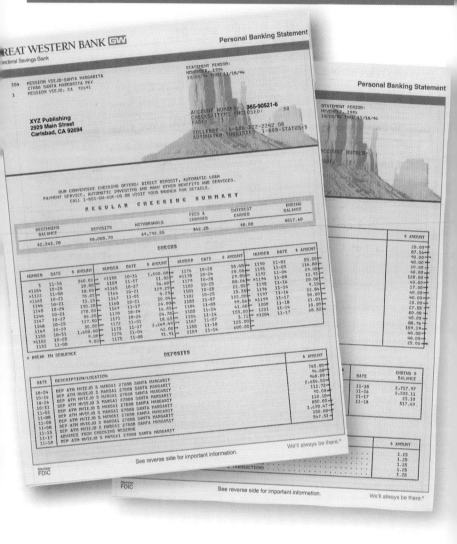

- **Invoices that have been paid** can be handled in two ways. Either move them to the customer's financial file, or keep them in a separate chronological file.

- **Bank statements and checks** are usually stored in boxes designed specifically for that purpose—office supply stores carry them. Reconciliation statements can either be kept with the statements and checks or in a separate file. Either way, they should be readily accessible for when you need to verify bank activity.

- **Receipts of sale** are generated by retailers, wholesalers, and manufacturers. If you own a small retail business, you might want to keep the daily receipts in a bank-statement box, as described above. Documentation for goods sold to wholesalers or manufacturers should be kept in the specific customer's file and in a chronological file.

- **Expense or time reports** for work you've done may be attached to your invoice and filed with it.

Managing Cash Flow

There can be many reasons for a monthly cash-flow statement ending in red ink. Your business could simply be unprofitable. Perhaps you're paying too much for raw materials, or maybe an inefficient manufacturing process requires you to hire too many people, thus inflating your payroll. Or maybe your expenses are exactly where they ought to be but you're simply not generating enough sales to cover your basic operating costs.

But what if you have a profitable business and your bank balance continues to plummet? Perhaps it's because you pay your bills on time, but your customers don't. Your money flows out, but the money owed you doesn't flow in.

There are two business practices that will help get the red out of a profitable company's cash-flow statement. First, unless your supplier offers you a discount to pay early, don't! Hold on to your money as long as you can. Second, collect every dime that's owed you on time.

Staying on top of your finances pays off.

? Who should manage your cash flow?

Without a doubt, the most important way you can increase your cash flow is to have the right person collecting the cash. Collecting your receivables is not a side job for your bookkeeper. Hire someone specifically for this critical task.

? What kind of person should you hire?

A good collector is part accountant and part detective. Often, he or she must reconstruct a series of involved transactions that took place over several months, determine the exact amount owed, then convince a customer to part with thousands of dollars. Therefore, a good collector must also be part politician and part bulldog. So when you start looking for someone to manage your accounts receivable, look for an individual who is assertive but tactful, thorough, organized, and a born problem-solver. Most of all, look for someone who is persistent.

Managing Cash Flow

Your collector should keep a written record of each call he or she places to a customer. This can be done by attaching a log sheet like the one shown below to the inside cover of each customer account folder.

CUSTOMER CALL LOG FOR: _____

Date	Person Contacted	Invoice Number	Amount	Discussion	Date to Follow-up

Be sure to review your receivables regularly—at least every two weeks—and become personally involved in the resolution of the more difficult collection problems. Remember, cash flow is your life-blood, and you must treat it accordingly.

Below are few more pointers to help you keep the cash flowing.

Start clean. Insist that orders are entered accurately. After all, you can't expect to collect your money on time if you shipped the wrong merchandise at the wrong price to the wrong address two months late. Clean orders are essential to prompt collection. Furthermore, be aware that some customers who are closely monitoring their own cash flow will use the smallest error as an excuse to delay payment for months.

Carefully consider who gets credit and who pays cash. If you do not collect payment on delivery, you are in effect granting credit to your customers. The decision about who gets credit and who pays cash should be made by a someone who is experienced in analyzing credit reports and financial statements. This is a job for a skilled professional.

Provide incentives for prompt payment. Offer a discount to those customers who pay early, and impose a late charge on those who pay late. Incentives such as this will not dramatically affect your receivables, but every little bit helps.

More Cash-Flow Tips

❒ **Check invoices and statements for discounts** offered for paying early or within a certain number of days. You will save money on your order.

❒ **Designate a regular date** or dates each month when you or your accounts-payable person will write checks for all payments and prepare them for mailing.

❒ **Set up a schedule of due dates for bills** and plan to mail bills so that, though they are not late, they do not arrive too early. You can code each envelope with a mailing date and place it in a chronological file for mailing on a specific date. Or create active files that represent the mailing dates for your payments. Then simply mail those payments on the specified date.

❒ **Choose a checking account that does not have a monthly fee** and pays interest.

Manage your money wisely.

❒ **Don't maintain large balances in the checking account.** Make your money work for you. Store excess money in a savings account, money market account, or in certificates of deposit, depending on how quickly you plan to use it. Then transfer the money to your checking account when needed. If your savings and checking accounts are with the same commercial bank, you can easily transfer funds by phone when you need them.

❒ **Negotiate 60 to 90 days of interest-free credit** from your suppliers, which is like receiving an interest-free loan.

❒ **Lease major equipment** when possible to avoid tying up valuable cash in an asset.

Managing Inventory

Retail businesses must deal with another facet in information organization that is closely related to financial matters: inventory management. For many small businesses, inventory management is simply a matter of going with gut instincts. But research shows that at least 80 percent of retailers who follow their intuition suffer from cash-flow problems. The reason: Their cash flow is jammed up in the unsold goods at the back of the store.

A business's inventory is a reflection of the buying decisions, customer satisfaction, and overall philosophy of the retailer. It's also a telling sign of his or her skill and business acumen. If you have too much inventory, you will be forced to have higher markdowns, and higher markdowns mean a higher cost of goods sold and lower profits for your business. On the other hand, if you maintain too little inventory, you limit your ability to increase your sales.

The goal of a successful inventory-management system is to maintain just enough inventory to meet demand—no more, no less. It's an art that can take quite a while to master, and it begins with understanding exactly how much you can afford to spend on inventory every year.

How much money should you invest in inventory?

Experienced retailers use a very simple formula to calculate how many dollars to invest in inventory:

**Annual Sales ÷ Turnover
= Average Inventory**

What is **turnover?** Simply speaking, it is the number of times an item or stock of items are sold in a fiscal year. In other words, it's how many times the inventory turns over. This number can vary, but a good rule of thumb for many retailers is four turns per year.

If you know how much you expect to sell in a year, you use the formula shown above to calculate what your average monthly inventory should be. For example, if you expect to sell $600,000 in the coming year at four turns, your average monthly inventory should be $150,000 ($200,000 ÷ 4 = $150,000).

Does this mean your inventory should be $150,000 every month? No, it means it should *average* $150,000. Your inventory in November and December should be much higher than in January and February. But when you plan your inventory dollars, it should average out to $150,000.

What happens if you get five turns instead of four? Let's do the math. $600,000 ÷ 5 = $120,000. That's an extra $30,000 a month you get to put in your bank account instead of in your store's stockroom. Over the course of a year, that's a $360,000 difference.

It works the other way, too. If you get only three turns, it'll cost you an extra $50,000 a month ($600,000 ÷ 3 = $200,000). That means you will have to take $50,000 out of your bank account every month to pay for the one turn you didn't get, and at the end of the year your bank account will be $600,000 lighter. Or, worse yet, you'll be $600,000 in debt.

The Power of Turnover

Supermarkets make more money on the sale of cigarettes with an 8 percent markup than they do on housewares with a 40 percent markup. The reason? Cigarettes turnover 26 times a year, but housewares turn only four times. Thus a million dollars in cigarette sales at 8 percent markup with 26 turns will yield 208 percent profit, versus 160 percent on a million dollars in housewares sales at 40 percent markup and four turns.

Staying in-stock on what sells

Turnover is important to the financial success of a retail business, and optimizing turnover is impossible unless you stay in-stock on what sells. The theory behind the 80/20 Rule we mentioned in an earlier chapter comes into play here as well.

The case of Sears, Roebuck and Company is an instructive example. Many years ago Sears discovered that about 5 percent of its stock generated about 50 percent of its sales. An analysis of the top-selling stock showed that consisted of basic items, like a carpenter's hammer in the hardware department, pant size 34 x 30 in the men's department, and white latex in the paint department. Appropriately, Sears dubbed these items *basic-basic* and instituted a program bearing that appellation. The company decreed that stores must be in-stock on these items at all times. They put a process in place to closely monitor each store's efforts to stay in-stock on basic-basic merchandise, and the results of these efforts play a significant role in the performance appraisal of the managers in every Sears store.

Filling the Gap

A San Francisco–area businessman needed a pair of blue jeans. Unfortunately, the first store he visited was out of his size. Shrugging, he went on to another retailer. That store, too, was out of stock. He went to a third store, then a fourth and a fifth. Frustrated, the man asked if his was an unusual size. To his surprise, he was told it was, in fact, the number-one selling size. That's why stores were always out of stock. The man recognized an opportunity when he saw one, and immediately made plans to open a retail store with one primary objective: Stay in-stock. The man was Don Fisher, and the store he started is the billion-dollar chain called The Gap.

More Tips on Managing Inventory

❒ **Use interstore transfers.** If you have more than one store, take advantage of the interstore-transfer technique. When a customer requests an item from one of your stores and you don't have it, rather than order that item from the manufacturer, transfer it from another one of your stores. This tactic means that each of your stores does not have to be fully stocked with all items. You just have to make sure that at least one of your stores has the item. Of course, if the item is very popular or a staple of your business, you will want to have it available in sufficient quantities in each of your stores.

❒ **Organize your inventory by customer demand.** Instead of organizing by vendor, organize by item type so that you can more easily determine what demand for a particular item is.

❒ **Order broad, not deep.** Order your stock in a variety of items, but not too many of any one item. That way you won't be stuck if something doesn't sell as well as you thought it would.

❒ **Buy on-demand items narrow and deep.** Once you have learned what your popular items are, you can feel free to overbuy them preseason.

❒ **Computerize your inventory-control system.** It is the easiest and most effective way to track what you're buying and what is selling. Create a database using inventory-control software and classify by customer demand, style, size, color, store, and any sales-trend information. You then can access information in a variety of ways. For instance, you may want to know how well the large, economy size is selling or who is buying a certain size of your product.

❒ **Keep careful track of inventory, both sold and purchased.** None of the above techniques will be much help unless you have up-to-date information on the status of your inventory at all times, which means maintaining those computerized files—scrupulously.

Remember: You must track your inventory through your sales. *Sales never lie.* They will give you the best advice you can ever get about what to buy, when to buy, and how much to buy.

Managing Data with Computers

9

You've already learned that there's no way entirely to avoid dealing with paper in your office. Now for the good news: Even though you must handle some paper, computer technology can streamline your business to a much greater degree than you might think possible. In addition to the financial data already discussed, nearly every type of document covered in the previous chapters can be managed effectively, and certainly more efficiently, with computers.

How can computers simplify your life?

Computers replace a hodgepodge of record-keeping procedures with one uniform system. Suppose your business takes orders on goods it sells. You or your employee records them on a phone pad first, then in the daily sales log, then in the receivables ledger, on the invoice, on a shipping ticket, and finally on a monthly statement. That's a lot of work.

With a computer, a printer, and good accounting and payables software, you can enter the information one time into a database and have it transferred electronically anywhere you want. Your computer can even prompt you to send invoices and monthly statements, which it will create and print. Using this type of system, you'll save time and money, handle your billing faster, pay your suppliers more quickly, and keep your clerical-help costs down. You'll also reduce errors, since the information is entered only once.

Advantages of Computers

If your business has departments—accounting, production, payroll—you can set up a simple local-area network (LAN) so that all your departments can access one another's information. You can maintain the privacy of certain files, such as payroll, by requiring a password to access the file.

? How can computers save you time?

Computers reduce the time and pieces of equipment required to perform a task. Consider a typical form letter containing some timely sales information and some figures. To create each letter, you or your secretary must type in a name and address from the rotary file phone list, calculate the figures on a desktop calculator, check spelling now and then in a dictionary, and finally type the addresses again on envelopes.

With a graphical interface program such as *Windows 3.1* or the standard Macintosh system and a word-processing program such as *Microsoft Word,* you can

❒ merge a computerized mailing list of names and addresses into the form letter

❒ address envelopes and mailing labels

❒ do mathematical calculations on-screen while you're working on the letter

❒ spell-check the entire document

❒ look for more interesting words with the on-screen thesaurus

❒ print out multiple copies of one letter

❒ make global changes in all the documents if you need to revise the letter

❒ preview the letter on-screen before you print it out

Advantages of Computers

Computers provide quick access to information while you are working. A good graphical interface program like *Windows 3.1* or the standard Macintosh system allows you to

- check a calendar for a date or schedule an appointment

- set an alarm to remind you of the appointment

- dial a phone number

- send or receive a fax

- calculate figures

- check an address

- address an envelope

- create a *macro* of an often-used address or phrase so that it can be inserted quickly into any document

- create, save, and delete files

- locate a file and insert it into your document if it needs to be included in the document you are working on

All of these tasks can be accomplished while the working document is on screen. If you have a modem connected to your computer, you can even arrange to have lunch delivered from a restaurant.

What about financial-data tracking?

Computers keep you up-to-date on tax and financial records. As we mentioned in chapter 8, with a good accounting-software package, you can enter information once and have it stored automatically in the appropriate files, journals, and financial statements. Some programs allow you to set up recurring expenses, such as insurance premiums, that will be updated automatically by the computer at the appropriate time. All you have to do is print the

needed files out in hard copy or give your accountant a copy on disk. Establishing routines for taking care of the financial-data entry for the business unquestionably will go a long way toward keeping you ahead of the game.

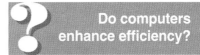

Do computers enhance efficiency?

Computers enable you to manage multiple projects. Computer software like Avantos Performance Systems' *ManagePro* will help you organize your projects and keep track of their progress relative to performance objectives. Like several other project-planning programs, this one is an integrated program, which means that information you enter in one area of the program automatically is available for use in another area.

Suppose your business goal is to improve sales by 10 percent this year. Using this program, you could divide this main goal into various sub-tasks for which you identify start and completion dates. You can also assign these tasks to specific employees. The program will automatically translate the dates into a time line that displays the status of each task. In this way, you can easily see when a particular critical task is not on schedule. You also could send notes regarding progress to employees or co-workers on their individual screens if your office were networked. Many types of customized reports are possible with a program of this type.

Computer Filing

How do you organize computer files?

An electronic database and spreadsheet will turn your computer system into a file system. With a computer you store information in exactly the same manner as you do paper files, but computers offer a host of additional features. The most obvious is that you can access the files much more quickly. You also can program your system so that if you make changes in one file, it will automatically update other related files that you designate. With a database spreadsheet you can establish inventory control methods, maintain information on clients, do sales projections, analyze unlimited business scenarios, and much more. As you set up your computer filing system, keep the following in mind.

Duplicate the organization of your paper files. Use the same filing conventions we established for paper files on computer files. For example, if one of your major file headings is *Contracts,* create a folder on your hard drive or floppy disk entitled *Contracts.* Then create files under this major heading, such as *Lease Agreement.*

Back up your files on hard disk, floppy disk, or tape. You must back up your files—especially important, irreplaceable files—on a medium other than the hard drive. Hard drives can crash, causing you to lose everything.

Save your files religiously. Whether you're working off the hard drive or a diskette, press the *save* key frequently. Some software programs have features that automatically save your work (or prompt you to do so) at regular intervals that you determine—every fifteen minutes, for example.

Keep your hard drive happily humming by getting rid of clutter. Just as you periodically get rid of clutter in your office, you should regularly delete any files on your computer that you no longer require, following the same guidelines listed earlier for paper files. This will speed up your hard drive. File compression and archiving utilities also can increase the space on your hard drive.

Computer filing pitfalls

The fact that there are no physical files in a computer system can take a little getting used to. Computer novices commonly stumble into two problem areas. The first is getting stuck in level-one filing systems. The novice creates a new file but neglects to put it in a folder (the equivalent of the hanging folder in the paper system). The computer automatically alphabetizes all the files so that the next time the novice signs on to the computer, he or she sees an alphabetized list of files. Soon, however, this list grows to be very long, and one tedious afternoon the novice must create folders for the various files and move them accordingly.

The second problem the novice faces is the opposite of not creating folders: creating too many of them. Because there are no physical constraints, you can create folders within folders within folders, resulting in a file system that's like a set of Russian nesting dolls. The drawback: You can't find anything! Sub-levels for each folder must be accessed individually, and if you leave them all open it makes the finder screen extremely cumbersome. To avoid the confusion, create no more than two levels of folders.

Virus Alert

Computer viruses can destroy files or incapacitate your system. Viruses are programs designed by computer hackers to jump from computer to computer by way of diskettes or networks. They can be merely irritating (for instance, replacing the word October with the word Halloween in every letter you write) or devastating (turning all your numbers into gibberish). To protect against viruses, install antivirus software in your system.

How can technology make you mobile?

it's compact enough to fit in your briefcase, if it beeps or clicks or has a little bitty screen, if it can translate English into twenty-five languages or just translate your handwriting into type, it's on sale in your neighborhood (or through a catalog). A mind-numbing array of computerized tools is available, all aimed at making you a lean, mean, travelin' work machine. For many people, this technology has completely revolutionized the workday. Chances are at least some of these tools can help you too.

Before you buy a portable computer or other electronic equipment, you should think carefully about what you really want to accomplish. Ask yourself how each item could benefit your work, what the drawbacks might be, and how much the product itself appeals to you. Don't underestimate the appeal factor. While it's a waste of money to buy every toy you desire, you're more likely to get work done if you enjoy the equipment you're using.

Portable Computers

The following are a few of the more popular items, but for a complete tour, take a visit to your nearest office-supply store (most are well stocked with computers, large and small) or to an electronics store.

Laptop computers

Also called notebooks and power-books, these increasingly popular computers are smaller than a phone book, lightweight, portable, and very powerful. Today you can purchase a 486 notebook that can run *Windows* software and weighs only five to seven pounds. Notebooks come with mono-chrome or color screens and as much as 545 megabytes (MB) of memory on the hard drive. Some have removable hard drives, which enables you to have as much storage space as you need. Notebooks range in price from about $1,400 to over $4,000, depending on features.

How flexible are portable computers?

Some people want the flexibility of using either their notebook or their office computer without having to transfer data by diskette. A computer docking station makes this possible. The docking station looks like a desk-top PC with a slot in the back for inserting the notebook. Once the notebook is in place, files can be transferred between the two computers. If you buy a docking station, make certain it can recharge your notebook batteries while the notebook is docked, and that the notebook can be locked into the station. (Notebooks tend to walk away on a regular basis.)

Laptop users often complain about batteries—they never last as long as the manual says they will. For insurance, you'll need an AC adapter and extra battery packs when you travel. This equipment will allow you to recharge at an electrical outlet in an airport or through the cigarette lighter socket in your car. Frequent fliers should keep in mind that you are not allowed to recharge batteries in the airplane's restroom. With so many people using laptop computers, the airlines were finding that the restrooms were the most popular place on the plane. It can take an hour to recharge a laptop, and that makes an awfully long wait for the lavatory.

As notebooks are prone to being stolen or lost, you should always back up your notebook hard drive onto diskettes. Or you can buy a portable tape backup, which can back up a 120 MB hard drive in ten minutes.

Tablets, palmtops, and pocket organizers

These amazing devices offer many of the features of laptops but weigh only two to three pounds. That's a lot easier to carry around than a six- or seven-pound laptop, particularly if you're carrying luggage as well. Some palmtops weigh as little as a pound and will fit into your coat pocket. Sporting 20-MB hard drives, some of these tiny computers can hold a memory card, much like a credit card, that allows you to trade data with other similar computers.

Pocket organizers will hold phone numbers, addresses, and appointments—some will even run spread-sheets and word-processing software. Others employ a touch-sensitive screen. You touch an icon, like the address book, and that feature is called up.

What is the Newton?

One of the latest devices to come into the market is the tablet-type computer based on the Newton technology from Apple Computers. It has a stylus for selecting menu items, drawing graphics, or writing longhand. Tablets are basically an electronic clipboard. As of this writing, all the bugs are not quite worked out of the Newton and its imitators. It can take anywhere from four to six weeks for the computer to memorize your handwriting, and until it does, some pretty hilarious mistakes can result. Some people believe the

Newton is the wave of the future, but as with any brand-new technology, it's not a bad idea to wait for the second or third generation before plunking down your cash.

Portable fax machines, printers, and modems

Once you've jumped in and bought a portable computer, a world of peripherals opens up to you. Nearly everything that can be attached to a regular computer comes in a portable, battery operated version too.

Portable printers are very popular peripherals. Most use ink-jet or thermal-fusion technology, both of which produce near–laser-quality printing.Don't expect these printers to operate as quickly or effectively as your office printer, however. They're best for emergencies.

Portable fax machines are also available. If you travel a lot and will need hard-copy documents sent from your home office, portable faxes could be helpful to you. (Most large hotels have fax machines anyway; you can always use theirs.)

An alternative to portable printers and fax machines is a phone jack and a fax-modem board inside your portable computer. They enable you to send your data to the nearest office fax machine over the phone lines and to receive data via the modem on your portable computer. These new mobile modems are as small as credit cards.

What are remote-access and remote-control software?

There are two ways to access your office computer when you're away from the office. The first is through **remote-access software.** Using a local-area network or a phone link to the office computer, you can access files from your office computer and manipulate them using application

software that resides in your portable computer.

Another option is **remote-control software,** which is valuable when the software applications you need to use require too much memory for a portable computer to handle. Your portable computer in this case acts as a dumb terminal for the office computer, which does all the work. You, however, control the operations from your portable computer.

With all these new devices at your fingertips, you can work any time, anywhere. But is that good news or bad? It depends on you.

The portables certainly make it harder to get away from work. When it's so easy to plug into your office from any location, you may feel compelled to work wherever you are. Consider a one-hour layover for a business flight. Without portables, you might read a newspaper or a novel or even go for a walk to clear your head. With a laptop and accessories, you may instead find yourself composing letters, writing a speech, calling the office to check messages, or fax-modeming a document back to the office. Of course, a portable computer is like television: You can always turn it off.

Plenty of people aren't very good at turning off work, however. If you own your own business, portable technology can be a blessing or a curse, depending on how driven you are. If you work for someone else, the same thing applies but with an added dimension: Your employer may now expect you to be working every spare moment. It's an old joke among professional women that the smartest thing men ever did was refuse to learn how to type. Not knowing how was a nifty way of avoiding a dreary task. Remember this as you run your fingers along the gleaming keyboard of that sale-priced laptop—if you don't own it, you won't have to use it.

As mentioned at the beginning of this book, many people today suffer from information overload—receiving more information than they are capable of processing. Portable computer technology can add to the overload and cause mental stress. The questions on the next page will help you determine if you're susceptible to information and accessibility overload. If you are, think carefully before buying portables.

Does Your Work Run Your Life?

1. Do you spend almost every weekend working in the office?

2. Do you have many business associates but very few friends with whom you socialize?

3. Do you take work with you when you go on vacation?

4. Do you check in with the office the minute you arrive at a vacation site?

5. Have you ever cut a vacation short to go back to work?

6. Do you find yourself talking only about work, especially in social situations?

7. Do you start getting anxious that you are not using your time wisely when you find yourself waiting a long time for a doctor or when stalled in traffic?

8. Do you always know what time it is?

9. Are you so serious and dedicated at work that you never take time out for sociable conversation with your co-workers or employees?

10. Do you feel under such constant pressure to achieve that you snap at your co-workers and employees because they don't seem to be doing their jobs quite the way you'd like?

If you answered yes to more than two of these questions, you may want to reread some of the suggestions in chapter 4 about getting away from work. If you answered yes to all of them, watch out! You could be on the verge of burning out entirely.

Remember, technological tools are just that—*tools*. They should not drive the way you work. Instead, as you better understand your work style and your goals, you can fit these tools into your working life so that they enhance your productivity and give you more leisure time. Their purpose is to liberate you, not enslave you! Used wisely, they can do just that.

Technological Storage

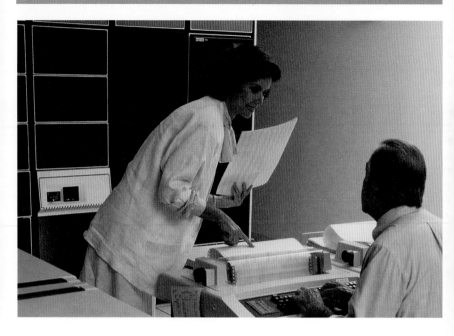

One aspect of the new technology is an unqualified winner: its storage capabilities. The longer you're in business and the more employees and customers you have, the more space you'll need to store all the documents your business creates and receives. Storage space is expensive, however, particularly if it is space that otherwise could be used as an office or to display more retail goods. Renting storage space outside your main office is also expensive, especially in urban areas. If you rent in an outlying suburb, every time you need the stored information you or an employee must take a field trip to fetch it.

Transferring your paper documents to other media will reduce the amount of physical space you need for storage. There are several ways to accomplish the information transfer.

❓ What is microphotography?

The technology commonly used to store data is called **microphotography** or **microfilming.** It is a process by which anything drawn, printed, or written is photographed and reduced in size, often to 1 percent of the original. The reduced image is printed onto rolls of film **(microfilm)** or sheets of film **(microfiche).**

Microfilm comes in a 35-millimeter or 16-millimeter roll of film that is read on a desk projector that returns the copy to approximately its original size. Microfiche sheets usually measure 4" x 6" and are read on similar desk projectors. In both systems, the projectors are often equipped with photocopying machines so that documents can be printed out in hard copy. Microfiche has the advantage of being easy to copy and fit into an envelope, facilitating the exchange of information.

It is now possible to link microphotography to computers to improve the speed and output of data retrieval. With computer output microfilm you can transfer computer data directly to microfilm, which is much faster and less costly than using paper.

The use of microphotography is constantly increasing in large and small businesses alike. Not only does microfilm and microfiche offer cost-effective options to paper files, but they also meet a new level of ecological responsibility, an area that many consumers are becoming increasingly aware of.

Using microfiche or microfilm, a business can reduce storage space by almost 98 percent. You can store 160 four-drawer filing cabinets worth of documents in one microfilm cabinet!

Digital reader-scanners also can reduce your information-storage space by allowing you to digitize images from film or print media and transfer them to a computer for processing and storage. You can take an existing document created by someone else and scan it right into your own computer in which form it can be manipulated on-screen just like any other computer document. This can save time and money in not having to regenerate an image. If your business generates an enormous number of documents, as law, medical, and accounting firms do, you may find it cost effective to purchase one of these devices and hook it up to your system for fast, easy computerization of this information.

Don't Forget the IRS

Always remember to keep the original paper version of documents pertaining to your taxes. The IRS can be very particular about your records and how they are kept.

There are very few businesses today that do not use computer technology in some form or fashion. This chapter has provided a basic overview of the computer options available to you, but if you're in the market for new technology, you need to examine the wares in person. The next chapter will give you some guidelines to follow when you go shopping.

10 Shopping for Technology

Computer technology evolves at lightning speed. Savvy industry people believe that a new generation of machines and software appears every eighteen months. If you love computers even a little bit, it's easy to be dazzled by all that's available to help you organize your office. But remember: The reason you should organize in the first place is to increase your business's productivity and your leisure time. The latest, fastest device with the most bells and whistles may offer more than you need to achieve that goal. Conversely, the bargain-basement PC clone may not be such a great deal when you realize it can't perform half the functions your business requires.

Inventory your business needs to ensure good match between your computer and your work.

market ensure that no matter what you buy in the way of computers, accessories, or software, it'll be considerably cheaper one year from now, which is a frustrating but unavoidable fact of life. You should, therefore, let your needs dictate the right equipment for you and the best time to buy, and resist the temptation to kick yourself later when you see your system on sale for half of what you paid.

When you're ready to buy, don't be shy about negotiating the best deal you can. For better or worse, many computer stores have a horse-trading atmosphere not unlike that of an automobile showroom. Shop around a lot before you make a decision, and if possible shop with someone who understands computers.

? How much will a computer system cost?

Just as technology evolves quickly, so prices tend to drop at an encouraging rate. The dynamics of such a fluid

106

Computerizing Your Office

Make sure that your employees are adequately trained on the programs they will be using.

Who will train you and your staff?

Any time you use computer technology to solve an organization problem, there are trade-offs involving training and maintenance. In most businesses with more than a few employees, one person emerges as the computer expert to whom everyone turns for advice. The role of computer whiz takes up a lot of time, however. If you don't want to buy a tutorial along with your system, realize that the employee who rides herd on your computer system won't be able to maintain his or her normal work load until the system is up and running. If you can afford it, you should purchase a tutorial and support service.

What is the best computer to buy?

The best computer for you depends on the size of your business and its organizational needs. A professional business such as a medical office, accounting firm, or law firm creates an enormous number of files of information on patients and clients. Their needs include

❏   easy access

❏   quick access

❏   a way to reduce storage space

❏   a method for transmitting data to other locations

❏   databases of technical information

These types of firms are quickly moving away from shelves of paper files to on-line databases and document-imaging systems that can store patient and client files and provide instant access to appointment schedules.

If you have a manufacturing plant or retail operation, your inventory must be managed, your sales tracked. The properly designed computer system can tell you at any time the status of your inventory and how that relates to the financial condition of your business.

CD-ROM and Networks

If you have a small business or are a consultant, your hardware needs will probably be less than those of a large company, but you could require as much or more software, depending on your field of work. Typical systems for large and small businesses are shown on pages 109–110. In additon to the standard items—printers, faxes, and so forth—many businesses are taking advantage of CD-ROM and national databases, or networks, to get an edge on the competition.

? What does CD-ROM technology offer?

With the advent of CD-ROM drives and access to national databases via modem, you can conduct research without ever leaving the office. (CD-ROM means compact disk–read-only memory.) By purchasing a CD-ROM drive to supplement your computer,

you'll be able to buy compact disks that hold enormous amounts of material—for instance, one disk can contain an entire encyclopedia. Many businesses add CD-ROM to their system in order to implement direct-marketing campaigns: The disks enable users to manipulate mailing lists as extensive as those of a direct-mail service.

? What are networks?

Computer networks provide *evolving* rather than *static* information. (Stock-market figures are evolving because they change daily; the information in an encyclopedia is altered only intermittently and so is considered static.) Computer networks also provide access to huge quantities of data similar to that available in a library—newspapers, periodicals, and so forth going back a number of years.

A Large-Business Computer System

In general, large businesses have the most to gain by installing the latest in computer technology. With this in mind (and assuming a generous equipment budget), their information-management system might look something like the layout below.

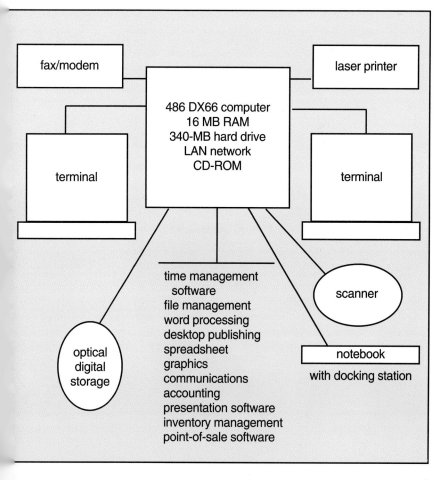

fax/modem

laser printer

486 DX66 computer
16 MB RAM
340-MB hard drive
LAN network
CD-ROM

terminal

terminal

time management
software
file management
word processing
desktop publishing
spreadsheet
graphics
communications
accounting
presentation software
inventory management
point-of-sale software

scanner

optical
digital
storage

notebook
with docking station

A Small-Business Computer System

Small- to medium-sized businesses that have limited equipment budgets can still take advantage of computer technology to speed the flow of information and decrease paperwork and paper storage. Yet don't be coerced into overbuying for your needs. The layout below depicts a system that can be purchased for $3,000 to $5,000. This system will handle most businesses' information storage and retrieval needs. Note the fax machine, which is absolutely essential in today's business world.

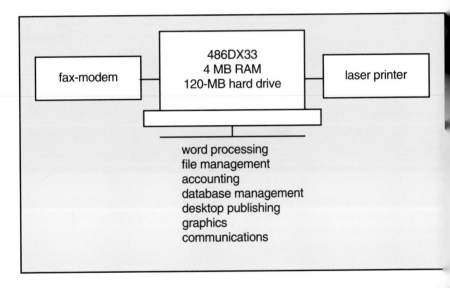

fax-modem

486DX33
4 MB RAM
120-MB hard drive

laser printer

word processing
file management
accounting
database management
desktop publishing
graphics
communications

More Computer Options

? What quality fax do you need?

The type of fax machine you choose will depend on how often you fax and on the quality of image your business requires. Simple fax machines have coarser image resolution, require more hand-feeding of material, and receive faxes only on special paper. More expensive models are faster, provide a better image, have more memory, and can be used with plain paper, among other features.

? What about fax modems?

Instead of purchasing a standard fax machine, it's possible to buy a modem attachment for your computer that enables you to fax computer files over the phone lines. These attachments are actually less expensive than a separate fax machine. But be careful. If you only have the capability to fax

computer files, you can never fax a brochure, or a photo, or an article you clip from a magazine—in other words, you can't fax hard copy. You can't receive hard copy, either. Some new computers contain fax-modems that *do* allow you to receive copy from a standard fax machine (it gets printed out on a laser printer). This function is very memory intensive, however, and it only solves half the problem: Unless you have a scanner with which to scan documents into your computer, you still can't *transmit* hard copy.

? Should you buy a fax or a fax modem?

At this time most businesses should purchase a regular fax machine. Get a plain-paper fax if you can afford it; if not, at least try to purchase a machine that automatically cuts the fax paper into separate sheets. Cutting twenty feet of fax paper into eleven-inch pieces is a real time waster and will try your patience over time.

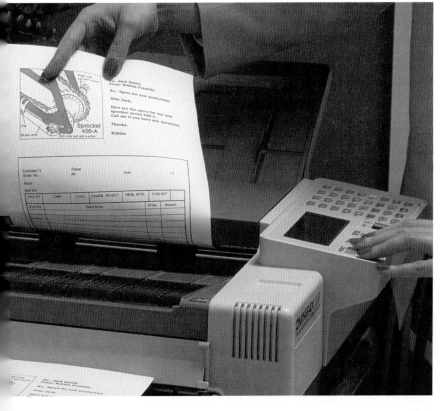

More Computer Options

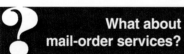

Extended Warranty/Product Protection Plan Available! See Page 184!

? What about mail-order services?

The cost of a computer system varies depending on how you purchase the components. There are myriad mail-order companies that will ship you any computer or accessory you need by overnight delivery. If you purchase from an out-of-state company, you pay no state sales tax, which can be quite a savings on an expensive system. Experienced computer owners often find that buying through the mail—particularly when dealing with well-established companies—saves them time and considerable money.

People who are not accustomed to setting up computer systems should keep in mind that some mail-order suppliers do not provide any sort of support—not even advice over the phone. On a complex new system, you definitely want support. Private computer consultants are one way around this problem, but, unlike consultants who work through the computer retailer, the private consultant has no incentive to make sure you're happy with the product, and his or her fees can be rather costly.

Organizing Onward

11

Organization, like business itself, is a pursuit that pays bigger dividends the longer you stick with it. If you're faithful to the techniques you've learned in this book, you'll discover that your office is running more smoothly, the crises are subsiding, and your confidence is soaring.

As you've seen, many people are intimidated by the information age. Others have long been told they're just naturally disorganized. The truth is, only a few of us are born instinctively knowing the best way to prioritize critical tasks or manage financial data. That's why there's a thriving industry of organization consultants ready to take over the chores—for a price.

It's better to organize your business or office yourself. Only *you* can decide which systems are right for you, which tools save you time and energy, which schedule brings out your creative spirit. When you develop the systems or play an active role in their development, you'll get an invaluable perspective of your business and the way work flows through it.

Once you've set up new ways of managing information and time, there's a lot of incentive not to backslide. After all, a well-organized file cabinet is much easier and more pleasant to work with than a stack of files on a chair. Still, old habits die hard, especially when a crisis hits.

Even if you let things slip for a few days or weeks, however, it will be relatively easy to get back on track if you've got a smart system already in place.

Each year will bring new technology, projects, and people into your business. If it's well organized, you'll incorporate the changes easily and increase your chances of success. Most important, you'll face the future enthusiastically, no matter how much traffic the information superhighway brings!

Resources

Books

AMA Complete Guide to Strategic Planning for Small Business. Cook, Kenneth J. Lincolnwood, Ill.: NTC Publishing Group, 1994.

Getting Things Done: The ABC's of Time Management, rev. ed. Bliss, Edwin C. New York: Macmillan, 1991.

How to Implement Information Systems and Live to Tell about It. Fallon, Howard. New York: John Wiley & Sons, 1994.

Manage Your Time, Your Work, Yourself, rev. ed. Douglass, Merrill E. New York: AMACOM, 1993.

Managing Information Technology in Turbulent Times. Fried, Louis. New York: John Wiley & Sons, 1994.

The Organized Executive: A Program for Productivity: New Ways to Manage Time, Paper, and People, rev. ed. Winston, Stephanie. New York: W. W. Norton, 1994.

Time Management for Unmanageable People. McGee-Cooper, Ann. New York: Bantam Books, 1994.

Where Did the Time Go?: The Working Woman's Guide to Time Management. Klein, Ruth. Woodbury, CT: Prima Publishing, 1992.

Magazines

The Office. Office Publications, Inc.; (203) 327-9670.

Supervisory Management. American Management Association; (518) 891-5510.

Videotapes

"Smart Solutions for Managing Your Time." *Inc. Magazine*, 1992; (617) 248-8000.

"The Melton Leadership System: Goal/Time/Stress Management-Flight 4004." National Education Training Group, Inc.; (708) 369-3000.

Index

Index

More Books in the Series

❑ *Office Design That Really Works!* is a user-friendly guide to help you make those difficult office design choices. This book will show you how to create and furnish you office spaces to maximize your business's productivity while keeping costs under control!

❑ *Computer Office Setup That Really Works!* takes the guesswork out of choosing the right computer system for your workplace. It will guide you through all your computer implementation decisions—from purchasing a system to obtaining the best possible results from computerization.

❑ *Business Communication That Really Works!* provides a comprehensive update on communications systems ranging from digital phones to cellular fax machines. The information superhighway is a friendly place when you're effectively using an on-line service and this book will show you how!

Illustration and Photo Credits

Illustration
Kersti Frigell: pages 3, 33, 39, 64, 65, 67

Photography
Apple Computer, Inc.: page 100

Comstock, Inc.: pages iii, vi, 1, 2, 4, 5, 6, 7, 8, 9, 10, 11, 12, 13, 14, 15, 16, 17, 18, 19, 20, 21, 22, 23, 24, 26, 27, 28, 29, 30, 31, 32, 34, 35, 36, 40, 41, 42, 43, 44, 45, 46, 47, 48, 49, 50, 51, 52, 53, 54, 55, 57, 58, 60, 61, 62, 63, 65, 70, 71, 73, 74, 76, 77, 78, 79, 80, 81, 85, 86, 89, 91, 93, 94, 95, 96, 97, 99, 102, 104, 105, 106, 107, 108, 109, 111, 113

Dome Publishing: pages 83, 84

Filofax: page 37

Great Western Bank: page 88

MicroComputer Accessories, Inc.: page 110

Pacific Bell: page 87

Plan-A-Month: page 38

Southern California Edison: page 87

Unocal: page 87

Notes

Notes

Notes

Notes